RENAISSANCE SWORDSMANSHIP

The Illustrated Use of Rapiers and Cut-and-Thrust Swords

John Clements

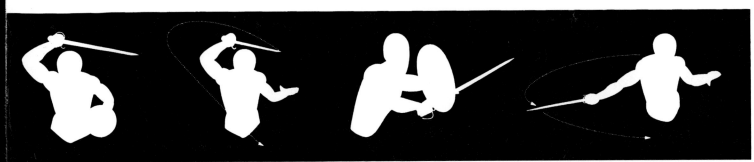

Paladin Press • Boulder, Colorado

Also by John Clements:
Medieval Swordsmanship: Illustrated Methods and Techniques
Masters of Medieval and Renaissance Martial Arts

Renaissance Swordsmanship:
The Illustrated Use of Rapiers and Cut-and-Thrust Swords
by John Clements

Copyright © 1997 by John Clements

ISBN 13: 978-0-87364-919-3
Printed in the United States of America

Publisher's Cataloging in Publication
(Prepared by Quality Books)

Clements, John
Renaissance swordsmanship: the illustrated use of rapiers
and cut-and-thrust swords and their use/
by John Clements
p.cm
ISBN 13: 978-0-87364-919-3

1. Fencing. 2. Swordplay. 3. Swords. I Title.

GV1147.C53 1997 796.8'6
QBI96-40837

Published by Paladin Press, a division of
Paladin Enterprises, Inc.
Gunbarrel Tech Center
7077 Winchester Circle
Boulder, Colorado 80301 USA
+1.303.443.7250

Direct inquiries and/or orders to the above address.

Visit our Web site at www.paladin-press.com

Contents

To all the nameless, faceless, struggling sword fighters. Never give up, never stop practicing, and never think that you're the only one who knows.

Warning

Neither the author nor the publisher of this work is responsible for any physical injury or damage of any sort that may occur as a result of reading and following the advice or instructions herein. Before attempting any physical activities described in this book, the reader should consult with a qualified physician. In any form of weapon sparring, always use safety equipment and, remember, *never* fence without a proper, regulation fencing mask. The information in this book is for *information purposes only*.

Preface

The purpose of this work is to serve as a short reference for sword enthusiasts and a guide to direct their study. It is intended primarily to dispel the many myths and misconceptions permeating the field of European swordsmanship and propagated by the media and entertainment. It is meant to serve as a source for all those people who over the years have asked, "What's a good book on Western swordsmanship?" To which I could only reply that there really wasn't much.

Therefore, this work is aimed at three audiences: (1) sword enthusiasts, who will welcome a work on their favorite subject, (2) novice practitioners, both individually and in various organized groups, who have for so long been without skillful guidance or a comprehensive reference, and (3) followers of Asian martial arts, who are sadly ignorant of their own Western martial heritage. To this we could also add a fourth: the complete neophyte who by reading this book may develop an interest and gain respect for what we all enjoy.

This work is not meant to be an all-encompassing "how to" manual on swordsmanship; in fact, it is far from it. Unlike other works on the subject, it was written from the perspective of and with regard to the historical function and use of swords. It approaches the material as a martial art and not from an exclusively military history perspective. This work is also not intended for fight choreographers, though they may certainly benefit from it.

This book is about swords *and* swordsmanship because you really cannot study one without the other. Although they have been presented that way again and again, doing so is like writing about cars without ever mentioning driving. For too long, swords and swordsmanship have been separated (luckily by authors who were honest enough not to try writing on a subject in which they had no experience).

Unfortunately, for most students of swords and swordsmanship, practically every book available on European arms and armor describes swords from a museum curator's point of view. That is, they describe merely the evolution of the weapons, paying particular attention to the craftsmanship, artistry, and hilt design. This typical approach is understandable because the authors are, for the most part, historians and not martial artists (how many of them have even handled, let alone used, the weapons they study?). They focus on form rather than function. Few of the works describe in any detail or accuracy the *why* of weapon design. What good does it do for a sword practitioner to know great details about pommel decorations or blade inscriptions but not know why a certain sword was fashioned that way or how it was used? Only a few references give information in this regard and usually only as it relates to the armor the weapons encountered. Although the influence of armor on weapons is important, such an exclusive focus is limiting and misleading.

Because there is no definitive reference to turn to, people are free to suppose whatever they want about European swords and their techniques, including making up countless theories that are ignorant of history, archaeology, or practical utility. People in this activity are notoriously afraid or unable to say "I don't know" about some aspect of swordsmanship.

This material originated from a series of discussions among friends and fellow practitioners. No one had all the answers, and many had serious misconceptions. After comparing anecdotes, sources, and experiences, I began to realize that far more research was necessary. Later, the accumulated information and experiences formed the basis of a series of classroom lectures and demonstrations. They, in turn, helped produce a more defined body of knowledge. It was not easy to avoid the haphazard trial-and-error approach, hearsay, and sheer fantasy currently permeating this field.

This work is the product of extensive (sometimes obsessive) research and hands-on practice in fencing, contact-weapon sparring, and training (far too briefly) with

historically accurate replica weapons. It was written mostly because no other such reference existed and one was very much needed. For too long I had longed for such a book. Finally, after years of disjointed research, personal study, and discovery, I realized that I was able to write it myself.

The focus of this presentation makes the historical lethality of sword fighting paramount and the modern recreational aspect secondary. As with so many of my kindred swordsmen studying today, my intention is to return historical fencing to more of a true martial art. It is my hope that this book encourages serious training and further exploration.

Gratitude for this work must go to my first fencing instructor, the venerable Sophie Trett; my good friend Todd Palmer; the late saber master Louis Bankuti; and especially my friends (and some not so friends) who have sparred and trained with me over the years. I must also give special thanks and appreciation to Hank Reinhardt of Museum Replicas for his sage counsel and wisdom over the years. I must thank all my loyal Nevada students, past Medieval Battling Club members, and those loved ones who tolerated my madness, particularly my dearest Pamela. I must also acknowledge all the many predecessors whose reference works are invaluable sources.

In a work of this magnitude, there are bound to be errors, and for those I must apologize. Often, our information is only as good as our sources and cross-references (and proofreading skills!). We must be prepared to accept most historical things as tentative, pending further investigation. They are rarely certain. All we can hope for is future confirmation or clarification and that we haven't repeated incorrect information. Martial knowledge itself must, in part, always remain theory. Sometimes, though, we must follow our instincts as we accept some material while rejecting other (precisely why neither historical research nor martial arts are exact sciences).

Introduction

"With 2,000 years of examples behind us, we have no excuses when fighting for not fighting well."

—T.E. Lawrence

There really is no such thing as a traditional European sword art per se. What does exist is a collection of reconstructed techniques and movements based on analysis and conjecture of historical arms, armor, art, and literature from a variety of periods. Unlike in the Asian martial arts, there is no traditional teaching method for Renaissance swordsmanship. However, there is no ritual or mystique either.

Because no real historical schools of European martial heritage survive to pass on their learning or tradition, enthusiasts have had to rediscover skills virtually on their own. There are a few manuscripts and instructional materials that have survived on Renaissance sword use, but most of what they offer is only rudimentary. Through interpretation of historical manuals, archaeological analysis and reconstruction of weapons, and pure supposition, many practitioners are trying to rebuild this lost knowledge. They will surely continue to do so.

Tracing the origins of sport fencing, reenacting battles, experimenting with safe sparring weapons, and contrasting Western experience with Asian martial arts have been the primary tools so far. Because all this can only take one so far, an important step involves dedicated, serious sparring. Some of the greatest insights have come from studying the actual historical weapons themselves and then doing hands-on practice and training with accurate replicas.

Of course, modern people doing research or reenactment can only hope to approach, not surpass, those warriors in history who trained practically every day to fight and kill with real weapons. Such men were warriors who passed on their experiences learned in life-threatening war over hundreds and hundreds of years. How can modern practitioners training intermittently or playing on weekends even imagine that they could duplicate this fighting skill? Who would presume to even dare innovate their own fighting techniques?

1

It has been said that the only way to truly learn the real way to fight and kill with a sword is to do it. The most that can be reasonably achieved is a facsimile of what the ancient warriors did. This can only be achieved through the advantages of safe contact sparring in which one can be "killed" and yet live to learn and improve from it. Sparring is virtually the sole means at our disposal for emulating the skills of the warriors of the past.

It is only through contact sparring and live-weapon test-cutting, not costumed theorizing and playing, that we can speculate on what appear to be practical defense and offense with a sword. By studying the weapons, armor, historical accounts of battles, and artwork of the period, we can come up with a reasoned interpretation of how men actually fought and killed with those weapons. This only takes us so far, and active sparring and training must then take over. Although it may not be for real, sparring and test-cutting use the same movements and teach perhaps the same physical mechanics encountered in real battle. Only the emotional challenge of facing death and taking life is, fortunately, missing.

That is not to belittle the importance of those factors—quite the contrary, for they are paramount. It is quite different from the friendly, sometimes honorable, and occasionally chivalrous encounters of modern enthusiasts (despite the intensity of competitions). Being threatened with pain, maiming, or even death must totally change one's outlook. The level of adrenaline increases, and the emotional responses of rage and fright come to the forefront. It is precisely the absence of those elements that enables us today to enjoy our "martial sport" and our research.

There is an immediate lethality to weapons that is not found in the unarmed martial arts. They were and are tools of warfare. Sword use is about killing. It is not about disarming, dissuading, discouraging, or even simply defending oneself. Despite all efforts at emphasizing philosophy, character development, etiquette, and artistry, the purpose behind a sword is self-evident. It is perhaps for this very reason, above all others, that skilled practitioners and knowledgeable instruction are so rare to encounter. The techniques of sword use have developed in history because of the necessity to defend oneself and defeat the enemy. The moves are those that the natural mechanics of the human body allow. It is a matter of physiology and psychology. The method of discovering, practicing, and applying the most effective and efficient of these (against someone else doing the same) is what we wish to study in the form of our Western martial heritage and the skills of Renaissance fence: the *Art of the Sword*.

Author's Note

In this work on Renaissance swordsmanship (roughly 1500 to 1700 A.D.), I have chosen to present information on the later rapier first and on the earlier cut-and-thrust form second. Despite the fact that the rapier and its method were developed from the cut-and-thrust form, I believe that presenting them out of their historical sequence has certain benefits.

The rapier form is much more familiar and has been the victim of simple misunderstanding and myth. The cut-and-thrust form, on the other hand, has been largely ignored and will appear new to many readers. It requires more careful definition to distinguish it. I believe it is easier to go back and contrast the cut-and-thrust form with that of the rapier after the reader has become more thoroughly acquainted with the cut-and-thrust form. I also believe that this will create a better appreciation of the value of the cut-and-thrust style and its differences from both the rapier and even the medieval sword. In re-creating the rapier method, we cannot just trace it back from modern fencing alone: in many ways, this

is a backward approach. Instead, we should start at medieval fighting and then look forward through the cut-and-thrust method from which the rapier *actually* came.

Renaissance swordsmanship certainly did not jump overnight from a medieval "hack-and-slash" mode for the battlefield to the rapier's thrusting, fencing style for self-defense in urban settings. There was a definite and recognizable transition form between the two. Books and films are full of innumerable depictions of knightly combat and musketeer-style rapier duels, but the cut-and-thrust form has been virtually overlooked. As well, museum curators and arms collectors have often failed to identify the cut-and-thrust form properly because of their overemphasis on hilts and guards rather than blades. It is a sword's blade that directly follows from its purpose and that dictates its manner of use. Practitioners today, examining historical manuals and training with accurate replicas, have been able to gain practical insight into the transition form (partially by *not* following a strictly modern fencing interpretation). This, in turn, has helped provide a greater understanding of the evolution and use of the rapier.

In the course of studying the rapier, one explores the use of such items as daggers, bucklers, and grasping gloves, and it becomes clearer how they related originally to the use of the cut-and-thrust sword. From this an understanding can be drawn of just how these two methods are so often erroneously and neglectfully fused. Telling the difference between Renaissance swords that are true rapiers and those of the cut-and-thrust variety is not hard. First, we can examine the blade's width, thickness, and edge. Second, we can handle it. Only by following these two steps can we determine whether a sword can be used for effective slashing and cutting moves or for rapier techniques—but not both. Because of the variety of Renaissance sword blades, this is just as subjective now as it was during the Renaissance. One cannot make assumptions about use without substantial familiarity with fighting, fencing, and cutting.

Although more closely associated with the medieval period, the two-handed sword actually saw its fullest development and greatest use during the Renaissance. In spite of this, I have chosen not to include any material on the two-handed sword because it is a battlefield weapon and not directly related to the civilian use of the rapier and its earlier cousins. There is clearly not the level of misunderstanding surrounding two-handed swords as there is with rapiers and cut-and-thrust swords. The two-handed sword is probably less well known in the first place and so, there is less to get confused about. This book is not about Renaissance warfare or even battlefield fighting. So in this one sense alone, this work is not a complete or exhaustive study of all manner of Renaissance swordsmanship.

Additionally, I must admit that I do not have sufficient experience with the weapon to feel I can do justice to an accurate description of its use during the period. I have also not found consistent or reliable sources elsewhere. Attempting to include the weapon would have also entailed describing the use of similar medieval weapons and how the two-

handed sword differed from them. That would be well beyond the scope and focus of this effort. I can also add that while there were certainly other sword types used on Renaissance battlefields (such as the *schiavonia* or the close-quarter *katzbalger*), these two were excluded from this study. These forms of wider-bladed shorter swords really did not represent any major change in, or development of, swordsmanship over that of previous centuries as can be seen in the transition to cut-and-thrust or the development of the rapier.

As with cut-and-thrust swords and the rapier, use of the two-handed sword was, of course, taught during the Renaissance. Some schools are known to have included it in their fencing curriculum, and there existed others using it exclusively. They instructed not only in its obvious battlefield applications, but also for private dueling. The German *Marxbruder* fighting guild, established in the late 1300s and lasting into the 1600s, came to specialize in two-handed swords. There are some historical manuscripts that give an indication of how this was conducted. *Talhoffers* famous Fectbuch describes some methods of using these huge weapons, which were made most famous by the German mercenary *Landsknechts*. A personal duel with two-handers must have involved a great deal of sweeping blows and weapon banging on weapon. In this way, it seems very similar to the "rough and tumble" sword-and-buckler brawls. Interestingly, there are in fact some references to instructions on how to handle two-handed versus cut-and-thrust-type swords and even the odd occasion of rapier versus two-handed sword. We do know that there were techniques for using it almost like a staff weapon, a club, and even a spear. Blows could even be struck with the hilt while holding the blade.

When creating the illustrations that follow the text, I made an effort to avoid as much stylistic influence as possible and merely to display the mechanical application of techniques or concepts in their proper tactical context.

CHAPTER ONE

The Rapier

The rapier sword and its unique method of Renaissance swordsmanship are rarely understood or fully appreciated. Therefore, some basic facts need to be established.

Although the rapier and its related swords have a familiar appearance and recognizable style of use, there seems to be a lot of general misunderstanding about these weapons. This misunderstanding, ranging from simple mistakes to ignorance and virtual delusion, has a number of origins. The rapier is synonymous with swashbucklers and Renaissance cavaliers as seen in *Three Musketeers* and *Zorro* films and a wide range of classical stage plays. The weapon has gained popularity at the cost of misinterpretation. The sport of modern fencing (particularly with the épée) with its distinct weapons and sporting rules, though based on a historical model, is different in form and function from a rapier duel.[1] Additionally, the rapier is a weapon altogether different from its

ancestor and Elizabethan "cousin," the cut-and-thrust sword. The two are closely related but used differently.

A great many people are under the impression that rapiers can be used to slash and hack so as to dismember and even decapitate. This misunderstanding is partly the result of the influence of movie fencing. The choreographers of the vast majority of films and shows have the actors, unskilled in swordplay, making relatively "safe" slashes at each other. This is done to avoid dangerous thrusts (can't have them stabbing so near each other's face). Instead, we witness the actors performing all manners of wild cuts right out of the Middle Ages—cuts that would get them killed in a real rapier duel. Those who also believe that merely running the blade, or even the tip, over an opponent's clothing would make it cut into their flesh are mistaken. The influence of Hollywood leaves many with the impression that rapiers are intended for slash-and-cut use. This is inaccurate.

It is perplexing why so many people, the

majority of whom do not even own accurate replica rapiers, make all manner of assertions about the sword's cutting ability *without ever having even practiced test-cutting with one*. Still more confusion is added by self-taught theatrical fencers doing what is essentially "noncontact" fencing. Choreographed, staged bouts, though occasionally well done, are rehearsed and artificial. They are about creating illusions to entertain the uninformed. Movie and show fights are equally notorious. Actors and performers are not trying to make body contact, and they do not have to avoid being struck by someone attempting to do the same. This is a significant difference—the one between showmen and martialist swordsmen.

Another reason there is so much misunderstanding seems to come from the multitude of wide-bladed, heavier, broadsword-type weapons that exist.[2] These kinds of cut-and-thrust "transition" blades—from the medieval to Renaissance periods—suggest a capacity for strong hacking cuts while their hilts, reminiscent of rapiers, imply thrust-style swordplay (one type, the Spanish *bilbo*, even has a cuplike hilt). They have compound guards or complex hilts and look similar to rapiers (with decorative, swept hilts, branches, and side rings). But swords of this type cannot be used in exactly the same way as true rapiers.

These transition swords reveal the trend toward killing by thrust and emphasis on "in-line" or point-on parrying.[3] As this trend introduced new fighting techniques, primarily in Spain and Italy, it also simultaneously influenced the design of weapons. This, in turn, further encouraged new techniques (a circle repeated often in the history of arms and armor). The "evolution" to the rapier and its style of swordsmanship developed out of the innovation of new techniques as much as from a new weapon itself.

Contrary to what is usually assumed, the rapier did not appear overnight. Its form developed from those leaner, compound-hilted, cut-and-thrust style civilian blades, which had themselves descended from the battlefield swords of the medieval period. The men who developed the rapier had to have been quite familiar with the cut-and-thrust swords of their day. These significant facts are clear from both the historical weapons themselves and the proper interpretation of period fencing manuals.

In a sense, the rapier is merely a classification of the Renaissance thrusting sword.[4] In fact, they have been described as being essentially just long, pointed metal bars attached to a hilt. The accepted hypothesis is that the weapon is of Italian origin, from sometime in the early 1500s. As with most sword types, there was no "standard" form of a rapier.[5] Rapier blades did vary, with some being slightly wider and others being more slender. Their general characteristics, however, were the same. Usually their edges were barely sharpened, though this seems to have varied depending on their width (earlier ones retained more of their edge).

Despite the narrow and obvious nature of rapier blades, many seem to believe that true rapiers can cut almost as well as wider cut-and-thrust swords—or even as well as medieval swords! This is a fallacy due to a number of factors. Part of the problem apparently stems from the influence of sport saber fencing. In such fencing, the cuts are highly modified for safety; they are delivered from the wrist and elbow to limit their force. The fencing saber is a pseudo-weapon; real sabers are much wider and much heavier.[6] They also tend to have more pronounced curves.

Fencing sabers, on the other hand, are light, flexible, and very narrow with barely any noticeable curvature. They have their thin shape only for safety's sake, and any resemblance to sabers (or true rapiers) is therefore coincidental. Yet, the modified cutting techniques in saber fencing are obviously being applied by many people using épées as pretend rapiers. It is hard to understand why people would believe that a thin rapier blade, swung from the elbow, could make strong cuts (even a medieval sword, designed for real cutting, could not do so if used in this manner). To be honest, these individuals are not rapier fencing, but merely using épées for freestyle "dueling" or theatrical combat and calling it "historical" or "authentic" fighting.

A popular weapon catalog often offers a form of "sword-rapier" that many people have mistakenly referenced as "proof" about how rapiers could cut. This begs the question of why such a thicker, wider-bladed rapier, over all the others, would happen to be designated as a thrusting-and-cutting version. It also ignores the fact that there are so many other thin-bladed ones. If thin rapiers can slash and cut, why then have wide-bladed versions in the first place? In the same manner of thinking, if wide blades can thrust and move as well as thin ones, why would the thinner version ever have been developed? Surely not simply to reduce weight, else this would have applied to all sword forms.

It has been said that efforts during the Renaissance to make swords with the ideal elements of thrusting and cutting met with "various degrees of success." With a different cross-section, these weapons reportedly handle more slowly and stiffly than true rapiers. It's said that they neither thrust as quickly as lighter ones nor cut as well as heavier, wider swords.[7] The attempt to combine cut-and-thrust sword elements with the rapier's effectiveness produced weapons that lacked the rapier's overall speed and balance and were also less capable than sturdier cut-and-thrust blades. They are sometimes called "sword-rapiers," though this is a collector's term, not a historical

one. This is an example of people confusing cut-and-thrust swords with rapiers. It is the major misunderstanding at issue. It only makes sense when we understand that rapiers do not cut well and that wider-bladed swords, being heavier, are not as agile for thrusting. Those in between do neither very well, or at least not well enough to favor one. This would explain why specimens are so rare. Swordsmen at the time may have learned to prefer either a sturdy cutting blade or the new, faster long rapier.

Visual inspection of rapier blades easily reveals that their diamond-like shapes are physically incapable of making deep, shearing cuts. This is precisely why edges on other hacking-cutting blades are wide and thinner. The actual "edge" of a rapier is fairly limited and sometimes not even sharp enough to make lacerations or prevent it from being grabbed by the bare hand.[8] By being relatively thick edge-on, in order to be thin, yet strong, the rapier's blade's angle is not able to make deep cuts. Being thinner, the rapier requires a shape that is not as flat as other swords (the primary reason it also had to be strong and well tempered). Many decorative imitation rapiers do not even attempt to simulate their true shape (or weight), and this too misleads the uneducated. A rapier's edge also takes considerable abuse in sliding, gliding, and smacking, which, again, limits the sharpness of its edge.

Swords are designed according to how they are going to be used. To cut, a sword requires an edge at a very acute angle, and the blade *cannot* be too thick. It is a sword's blade width and edge angle that determine whether it can be used for cutting. A true rapier is a tip-based thrusting sword that works by stabbing and piercing, not by cleaving. Certainly, some versions can make draw-cuts. For instance, if a sword is placed against an inner elbow, back of the knee, or the face or neck, a quick sliding motion would tend to incapacitate a foe. But this slicing potential (using only the tip and first quarter of the blade) is far from killing with a cut. The weapon is incapable of delivering edge blows that cut.

For example, a rapier slice against the chest is not going to cut into the pectorals or even come close to entering the ribcage. This also applies to the abdomen, collarbone, or sides. It would hurt if it managed to penetrate a doublet (jacket), but would do little else. Against a shin, however, a slashing rapier will also not penetrate the bone, whereas a cut-and-thrust type of blade could.

In rapier combat, if the arm is raised to deliver a slash or make a wide parry, it will almost always expose the body to a quick counterthrust or riposte, as in modern fencing. Attempts to slash, as with a medieval sword, will quickly result in the fighter being "run through." Even if a rapier slash connected, it would likely not do enough damage to stop the adversary from making his own lethal thrust in reaction. Examination of the historical rapier (not cut-and-thrust) fencing manuals support this.

For the most part, cuts are just plain slower than thrusts. The speed with which a rapier can be used allows its movement all around the guard of heavier swords, "disengaging" back and forth and making it nearly impossible to defend with a slower weapon in the typical manner. Its long reach—on average, more than three feet of blade alone—made defense even harder.[9] As fast as a rapier is on the thrust, it is equally quick in its withdrawal and thereby able to continually renew attacks.[10]

The ascendancy of thrusting over cutting, it must be emphasized, refers far more to single combat than to battlefield conditions of mass warfare. This is an important distinction. Although a longer rapier has a reach advantage, too much length makes one heavier, slower, and

harder to handle if not outright self-defeating. When the lunge and parry/riposte became more common techniques, blades shortened to a more "standard" length. The average appears to have been between 40 and 45 inches, but some were more than 50 inches. For the rapier fighter to defend against a slashing attack by a cutting sword, he had to be exacting in his movements. Slipping in an effective counterthrust took skill and confidence. Strangely enough, despite the rapier's speed, it is still possible to grab the blade with the hand (a maneuver obviously quicker than moving a whole sword to parry); this was commonly attempted when necessary and sometimes assisted by a heavy leather or mailed glove, known as a *guanta di presa* or grasping glove.

The rapier's thin blade allows maximum penetration by focusing power in a small point. This is the reason for that weapon's deadly thrusting ability. A mere pressure of only a few pounds of force could be enough to kill in this way. Potentially, effective thrusting kills can even be accomplished by a simple strong push of the weapon. Reportedly, tests on cadavers have apparently demonstrated the ease of puncturing. Historically, stab wounds were notoriously dangerous because they could not be treated like cuts. One could not tell how deep they were (and the wider the blade, the larger the wound). At the time, there was little or no knowledge of internal surgery or sutures necessary to stop internal bleeding. Death was not always instantaneous from rapier wounds; it frequently came later from blood loss or even long after from infection.

There is some debate over the overall effectiveness of a long, thin stabbing weapon (such as the effect on a fighter hit in the thigh or shoulder). Although historical accounts tell of fighters taking numerous minor punctures, it is

8

conceivable that someone could be run through and not have a vital area punctured. A dedicated cutting blade will deliver tremendously devastating and deep lethal gashes, but it is still possible (though unlikely) to receive a number of cuts and survive.

Provided that no arteries or tendons are severed and the muscle and bone remain intact, the human body is capable of taking severe lacerations and still keep going. This is apparently not the case with internal puncture wounds, including those from low-velocity firearms. A fast thrust placed as the opponent was, say, lifting to cut could easily end an encounter. A deep stab wound to the eyes, throat, or heart would kill instantly. A stab to the lungs, intestines, bladder, or sinus could also be mortal. It was not uncommon for cuts to the head to bleed into the eyes and disrupt vision. Of course, it is difficult to make generalities concerning wounds because the psychological makeup and physiology of the receiver are major variables. In this subject, this should always be kept in mind. If the depictions of thrusts shown in historical manuals can be believed, rapier stabs were horribly effective.

As a thrusting sword, the rapier took advantage of all this. By putting emphasis on thrusting kills (for efficiency and speed), one naturally finds oneself pointing the blade at the opponent. This is one of the main differences between a rapier and a cut-and-thrust sword. The "on-guard" position is point-on and not with the weapon held back, angled high or tip raised. Fighting point-versus-point necessitates blocking the attacking thrust while countering with your own. Rapier techniques inherently use counterattacks in the manner of simultaneously preparing for (thrust) attacks as parries are made (a concept familiar in Japanese sword arts). Its ability to riposte (counterattack) can be quick and

effective. At the time, this development was a novel idea and not completely accepted.[11] To many, use to the traditional hack-and-slash swordsmanship of the day, the new weapon appeared weak and its method practically useless.[12]

It needs to be realized that fighting tactics come from techniques, and techniques are derived primarily (though not exclusively) from the mechanics of the weapon itself. This is the source of rapier fencing moves. As well as suggesting a leaner stance, perhaps more so than with other sword types, it places a direct and heavy importance on footwork, i.e., agile and efficient movement (this is something virtually ignored by most novice historical-combat practitioners). Since it is held essentially horizontal (in order to use the tip predominately), the blade necessarily must be somewhat lighter, which means being thinner. This, of course, follows from its method of piercing attack. Improvements in metallurgy at the time had allowed for a stronger, thinner blade as well.

With a rapier, the standard stance or ready position is somewhat tighter than that of a cut-and-thrust sword (which itself was only altered from the earlier medieval "sword and shield" form). It resembles more a boxer's stance, allowing for slips, quick stepping, and explosive lunging. It is similar to, but not quite exactly like, that of modern fencing with its very linear stance (taken not so much to refuse potential targets for the opponent but to allow one's sword arm maximum reach). It is tighter, not nearly as "sideways" and the knees are less bent. The fighters are closer together and, unlike sport fencing with its restrictive, linear range and safety rules, rapier fighting provides ample opportunity for traverses (side and cross-stepping)—even more so when a dagger is used in the other hand.[13] This is sometimes called fighting "in the round" (only starting with the small-sword in the 1700s did duels begin to be fought linearly). Additionally, the stance may lead with either leg depending on the techniques being executed.

The second hand is not held out of the way, as in fencing today, but ready if necessary to deflect or slap incoming attacks (better to risk a hit in the hand or arm than one in the body). It is significant that once a sword is used one-handed without a shield, the lead leg typically becomes that of the sword-arm side (i.e., right-handed therefore right-legged). This naturally increases the reach of one's weapon arm while pulling the other side of the body slightly away from the opponent. This position changes the style of fighting and provides for different movements and footwork (e.g., the traditional fencing "cat-walk" form of stepping).

The rapier is also held differently than earlier swords by virtue of its method of use. It is a single-handed weapon. It can't be held in both hands.[14] The grip is essentially held parallel to the wrist. Rather than being gripped in a "fist," it is designed so that the hand is more open and the fingers somewhat extended, as with traditional fencing weapons (the rapier's essentially nonlethal descendants).[15] The reason for this is tip control. It allows for stronger thrusts than with a fist grip. The hand is held in a position that resembles pointing your index finger (it also happens to be difficult to hack or slash with any real power from this position). The sword's point can be better manipulated by wrapping the index and second fingers around the guard (sometimes called "fingering" and used in the Middle Ages and perhaps further back). Unless additional guard pieces were put in place, doing so exposed the finger. Because of this, some maestros advised against the practice. The unsharpened portion of the blade that the finger wrapped around became known as the ricasso sometime in the mid

or late 1500s. It became almost an extension of the rapier's handle.

The added control that inserting a finger over the guard or around the ricasso gives can be easily demonstrated. First hold a cruciform-hilt (cross-guard) sword in a typical "fist" grip; then hold it by wrapping the index finger over the guard. You can instantly feel the additional, yet subtle control that it gives to thrusting and parrying with the blade held horizontal. This only makes sense when your style of fighting begins to emphasize tip work and more linear fighting. Instead of "step, hack, step, slash," swordsmanship with the rapier became one of "in and out, back and forth."

With other sword types, the grip is more of a fist with the wrist relatively straight and the hand free to shift somewhat. With the rapier, the enclosed bars and cages appropriately restricted the hand into the pointing position. This was acceptable because the means of using the weapon did not require the hand to shift; only the fingers are left free to move. This also further illustrates the weapon's inability to be used in a strong cutting motion, as the hand is just not in an appropriate grip for such. Earlier cut-and-thrust swords must have begun to enable the grip to be held in both the fist and the more pointing positions. This was significant in allowing more thrusting action and in-line defense. Additionally, frequently using the tip compels the sword's balance to be slightly more toward the hilt (which, again, may help explain the advent of heavier compound guards). Centering the weight in the hilt allows the tip to be moved more quickly—something crucial in a thrusting weapon.

In keeping with this, we can see in the transition swords signs toward more rounded handles as opposed to earlier oval or flatter ones (this was most likely for ease of manipulation with the newer grip). The rapier also tends to have a noticeably smaller pommel, often with decidedly elongated or oval shapes. This is due again to how the weapon is held (as well as fashion). A larger shaped pommel would interfere with the new gripping method. Additionally, a large, heavier pommel was likely no longer required as a counter balance, since the complex guard was now itself heavier.

Certain early cut-and-thrust swords have "finger rings" or small crescent loops on their guards. These are the forerunners of the "arms of the hilt" (or incorrectly the *pas d'âne*) and later complex guards with their intricate and decorative branches.[16] Such guards were developed to protect the hands that were more directly in the line of attack, as well as to catch or trap an attacking thrust (which may or may not be a good thing to have happen).

Compound hilts of decorative shapes and designs are common features of both cut-and-thrust swords and rapiers, often leading to mistaken identity between them. These hilts provide obvious hand protection, perhaps, at first, less against thrusts coming in-line with the guard than from cuts and collisions with a foe's blade.[17] They could also entrap and break a thrusting blade. Swept hilt designs were numerous and varied more due to fashion than function. Fully encased cup-hilts offering total defense from thrusts (as with modern fencing épées) first appeared around the early 1600s, developing out of shell-like plates on the guards. Their weight was often reduced by decorative perforations (such as in Flemish Pappenheim rapiers). The cup hilt was a natural extension of plates attached to the bars, eventually forming into a single piece.

Despite its "modern" sporting descendants, rapiers were not exceptionally light weapons (ranging from two and a half to three pounds, with the earliest versions being heaviest). They are just too heavy to do many of the moves common to modern fencing. Yet, they can do things a heavier blade cannot. Rapier combat was certainly not as quick paced as modern fencing for this very reason.[18] They were also not nearly as flexible (although a well-tempered blade will always need a good degree of flex to keep from breaking). Sport fencing weapons are far more flexible, because they have to bend for safety, not penetrate. They are also much lighter than rapiers, and this may further explain why some enthusiasts, easily able to swing them, incorrectly believe they could slash in a rapier fight. The rapier sword was not nor cannot be used in exactly the same manner as modern fencing weapons.

It must be mentioned that the rapier was not a true "field" weapon (unlike the cut-and-thrust sword variety), but rather for "civil defense." The rapier was in a sense, the first true civilian weapon for personal self-defense (if one discounts tools such as knives). It can be considered more of a "town sword" as opposed to a "war sword." The rapier was not aimed for use in battle, where its limited cutting capacity and slender design make it vulnerable, but in "duello" (single combat) and skirmish. It has gained the reputation as *the* dueling weapon. Since its main killing threat is the tip, one cannot fight by freely cutting in multiple directions. It is not easy in the rush of battle to be able to deliver a lethal or incapacitating wound with one. The motion of extending to stab momentarily ties the blade up, making action against multiple attackers hazardous (but possible). This is often the dilemma of linear-based weapons. Also, in the crowded clash of battle, it can be broken by weapons that heavier blades would easily have blocked—thus another reason other sword types coexisted and survived beyond the rapier. The rapier certainly has its advantages, but it also has certain disadvantages, such as when facing larger shields, certain pole weapons, or heavy armor (all things it was not required to do). *What a rapier really does best is fight another rapier.*

Originally, the rapier was predominantly used by the lower classes. It became the sword of choice for encounters in back alleys and taverns (in other words, streetfights). Later it became the weapon of choice for the aristocracy and socially mobile, particularly on the dueling field (furthering its popularity).[19] Its techniques also relied somewhat more on careful, calculated thought than pure ferocity and power. This was in keeping with the new enlightened "sciences" then coming into vogue.[20] The conditions under which the rapier developed were particular, and as with any weapon, there are certain conditions under which it works best. Of course, this does not invalidate skill with it under other circumstances.

The rapier was almost always used with a companion weapon, typically a parrying dagger, but ranging from cloaks for entangling and mailed gloves for grabbing and deflecting to scabbards and even tankards. Again, this was primarily because the weapon is lacking in offensive cutting power (although the use of a shield, buckler, and dagger with cut-and-thrust swords was already common). The rapier naturally favors distance attacks over close-in or "cutting distance" encounters. Once close in or moved off-center, it has virtually no offensive capability and leaves the user a bit vulnerable. After all, the rapier was worn at a time when one did not go about carrying a large shield through town. Many rapier fights must surely have used much kicking, punching, grappling, and anything else that was possible.

Parrying in-line with the blade of the weapon gradually came about as techniques were refined. It was also made possible by having better and lighter, more maneuverable weapons. Parrying is done with the outside or bottom edge of the blade as opposed to the back or flat as with other sword forms. It has been surmised that improved parrying defense, and the resultant capacity to riposte better, eventually gave less reason for using a dagger with the rapier. A simple but quick movement of the rapier blade is enough resistance to parry another rapier's thrusting attack.

One might ask if the rapier's thin blade could be snapped or even cut by heavier swords and weapons, especially when blocking. The answer is yes, but that much is true about almost any blade. It can be surmised that rapier users, being reasonably aware of the weapon's relative deficiency in direct "resistance blocking," naturally developed moves that relied more on deflecting. The ideal (far more so than with other swords) is to cause the attacking weapon to slide off, pass by, or be pushed away rather than knocked, stopped, or bounced. To this, they made great use of evading movements as well as warding off potential attacks by the very threat of their thrust. This is not to say the thin rapier blade was not strong or capable of blocking (it would be practically worthless as a sword otherwise), but that one would avoid doing so when possible. Nor is this to say that other sword forms cannot use deflecting techniques. This undoubtedly has more to do with the simple efficiency of going for a counterthrust than any inherent parrying weakness.

What was also significant about the rapier over the older, more traditional cutting sword of the Renaissance was surely not only its obvious offensive agility, but its ability to effect a true riposte. More precisely, the crucial factor with the rapier was clearly that by being quicker, it could go from defensive to offensive action much more easily. After dropping its tip to parry, or after having its blade knocked or beat away, it can still manage to recover immediately. It is able to instantly return the point at an attacker. Through this, combined with lunge-like movements, its *counterattacking* potential is realized. It was plainly this dynamic that was precisely why its narrower, lighter blade was so much more effective in single (unarmored) combat than the wider cutting one. This quick, coordinated recovery power allowed the rapier to disconnect the act of parrying or defending from that of attacking. It was to develop (especially with the small-sword) into the idea of the true riposte, or a return attack after an *intentionally* separate and distinct parry.

The rapier's main effectiveness lay in its great speed combined with unorthodox, unpredictable movements and angles of thrusting attack —used in fighting unarmored adversaries. Although it is not an overall superior sword, in skilled hands it can be a frighteningly lethal weapon. This is particularly so when an adversary is unfamiliar with its use themselves. To the unknowing, it does not appear to be that dangerous or even capable of blocking without breaking. This is untrue on both accounts.[21] There is little doubt among rapier enthusiasts that those unfamiliar with the weapon's true potential (or with sport fencing in general) would have a challenging time fighting one.[22] Overall, the rapier is most effective against slower swords, shorter weapons, and where heavier armors are not a factor.

In this way, the rapier represents an innovative development in sword weapons.[23] The rapier users developed and advanced swordsmanship to a higher degree than had previously been seen in Europe. Speed and acquired accuracy were stressed over strength and stamina. Undoubtedly, the masters who developed the rapier's method were also quite adept already at the cut-and-thrust method and many instructional manuscripts on

swordsmanship were produced. The development of the various ready positions, warding stances, and parrying methods, besides being derived from cut-and-thrust forms, must surely have come about gradually from experiences of individual combat and from investigation in the established schools of fence.[24] With the rapier, thrusting techniques and in-line defense developed more than they had with any sword before. The idea of an exclusively thrusting sword was not entirely new, and there is evidence forms of it were known in antiquity. In another sense, rapier techniques are merely those a skilled user of a spear might employ, but on a much more precise, refined scale.

As with any sword, proper understanding of its use is required to have any effective skill with it. For instance, a poor fighter with a rapier, in spite of his formidable weapon, will likely lose to an excellent fighter armed with just a dagger. In the end, either weapon is just as deadly. Victory of one over the other is a matter of both the training and attitude as well as the conditioning of the fighter.

The basic techniques of rapier usage involve a great many stabbing extensions and lunging thrusts combined with threats and false attacks or feints (like in modern fencing). Quickness, accuracy, and grace are dominant characteristics. The agility of the tip to maintain a continual threat and potential counterattack even while blocking or defending is a major component of the weapon. This should be obvious; however, many untrained novice fencers attempting to slash or use them in a fist grip miss the concept entirely. Control of the point, attacking by thrust, and parrying or deflecting in-line are all arduous to master. They are not as obvious nor as automatic as hacking and slashing with a sword.

It has been said that making slashing cuts is more natural than thrusting because it uses the stronger and more instinctive movement of a striking hand. In contrast, thrusting with a weapon requires more deliberate thought and precision (even more so when a secondary weapon is included). This is clear even from how the weapon was carried. To ease its being withdrawn from its scabbard and quickly held point-on, it was worn hanging in a "sling" at about a 45-degree angle on the hips.

The rapier's "evolution" can be summed up easily. The less they faced cutting blades (fighters who raised their arms in attack) and the more they faced thrusting attacks, the less need fighters had for their own cutting edge. This resulted in three developments: their grips changed to reflect point-on handling; the protective coverage of their hilts increased; and to lighten them for greater maneuverability, their blade shapes changed at the expense of a true cutting edge.

Authors Turner and Soper put it best when, in the conclusion to their superb *Methods and Practice of Elizabethan Swordplay*, they describe the societal effect of the rapier in England: "Through the last quarter of the sixteenth century, the rapier passed from imported curiosity, to popular fad, to ubiquitous weapon. Though rarely mastered in its time and demanding a unique combination of skill, aggression, and cool-headedness, by 1600, rapier swordplay was highly prized and sought out as the ultimate fighting art by most sophisticated Elizabethans."

What is most important to realize is that the rapier is a different form of sword that involves different techniques. A cut-and-thrust sword can be used slightly like a rapier, but a rapier *can't* be used like a cut-and-thrust sword. Try and use a cut-and-thrust sword exactly as a rapier and you'll soon see the *need* for a rapier. Trying to use a rapier like a cut-and-thrust sword misses the whole point of

the rapier's unique techniques. Practitioners now are either simulating a true rapier or simulating a cut-and-thrust sword, not both. One is a lot heavier and *cuts*, and one is a lot faster and doesn't.

To clear up some of the misinformation and ignorance about these swords, the message about the rapier, its handling, and its true cutting power needs to be repeated. Rapiers are stabbing, piercing weapons and are not designed for making cutting kills. They kill by quick thrust and are demanding to both use and face—more so than the modern sporting variety. The true rapier is different from both the Renaissance cut-and-thrust sword and the later small-sword. It also represents one of the most innovative and original aspects of our European martial heritage. The record needs to be set straight and the many myths put to rest if enthusiasts today are to practice and re-create it accurately.

NOTES

1. The fencing weapon originates from what was a deadly and effective tool. Yet some say modern sport fencing (particularly foil fencing) is so far removed from its martial origins as to barely qualify as swordsmanship. It is no wonder that many sword enthusiasts find it lacking and dissatisfying or that Asian martial artists seldom appreciate it. There is a small but growing effort to return a more martial spirit to this elegant but overly refined sport.

2. Many of these are actually only modern decoration swords that have no historical counterpart and are, in fact, fictitious. They are quite impractical and have esthetic value only.

3. "In-line" here means in one line or with the sword pointed directly at the opponent and the blade held relatively horizontal and slightly angled. Primarily, the blade is moved at the hilt, rather than at the point, in order to block and deflect attacks.

4. The term rapier likely comes to us from the Spanish *espada ropera* (possibly meaning a dress sword—"sword of the robe"—or costume sword) and from the French *rapière* (first recorded in 1497 in the phrase *épée rapier* [source: *The Complete Encyclopedia of Arms and Armor*, Bonanza Books,

1979)). It could also be related to the Spanish word *rasper*, to scratch, or the German *rappen* (or *raffen*), to tear (source: "A Historical Guide to Arms and Armor," Steven Bull, 1991 *Facts on File*). It may have originally been slang. Surprisingly, the word was never used in Italy or Spain. The weapon itself was also generally unknown in Russia and many parts of Eastern Europe.

5. This is easily understood, given that medieval (and ancient) peoples had no mass communications or rapid transit. Ideas and fashion traveled slowly and were exchanged mostly person to person. Added to this was a conservative life-style of established custom and tradition.

6. A leading fencing coach once remarked that a brand of toy foam sabers handled almost identically to those of his sport. This is a sad comment on how much modern fencing has deviated from its heritage. Unfortunately, the only place we often see historical rapier use is with theatrical performers and stage shows. Even with many re-enactment troupes, one has to look hard under all their exaggerated and wild moves to see anything resembling realistic or effective technique.

7. Maybe some think of a sword blade essentially as a giant knife. This is incorrect; swords are not like giant knives. Compared with swords, knives for the most part have very different weights, balance, and flexibility, and also differ in their edges and hilts. They are not designed as swords or meant to be used in the same manner. A sword made like a knife would be far too heavy to use properly as a sword (as a great deal of the work of numerous professional knifesmiths-turned-swordsmiths has proven).

8. It's worth mentioning here that the term *razor sharp* for swords in general is somewhat inaccurate, as well as overused. Razors are "razor" sharp because they are so incredibly thin and delicate, *delicate* being the key word. A weapon that needs to regularly block and beat against other pieces of steel will, by nature, not maintain an exceptionally sharp edge. Even the virtually razor-sharp edges on fine Japanese blades, despite their strength, were still considered relatively fragile because of their hard, crystallized steel.

9. There was even at one time an ordinance in the city of London that prohibited rapiers of excessive length. Men seeking entry would have the tips broken off of their swords (thus effectively rendering the weapons impotent). This having been done to the weapon's point makes the most sense when we understand what exactly the rapier's method of use is.

10. There has, however, been some question about how much adhesion a body, particularly a falling one, would have to a blade being withdrawn from it.

11. Whenever radical transformations or just simple innovations with profound effects come into existence, it is normal for tradition and established custom to resist. This is notorious throughout military history. The rapier, being unorthodox, was rightly questioned and doubted. In the realm of swords and weaponry, potential and worth have to be demonstrated, not merely asserted.

12. Most famous of these critics were the Englishmen George Silver and his brother. In his 1599 book on sword use, the renowned Silver criticized and denounced rapiers as not viable in war and yet too dangerous to face in single combat. Though his argument has merit, a large share of sentimentality and whining can be detected in his complaint. Another swordsman, Sir John Smythe, published a work that criticized the rapier in 1590.

13. Although somewhat disparaged here, the sport of classical (collegiate/Olympic) fencing provides crucial fundamentals of movement and form that must be learned to develop any reasonable level of proficiency. The proper mechanics and concepts it teaches simply cannot be discounted by anyone seriously intending to take up rapier-and-dagger or cut-and-thrust swordsmanship. It has much to offer, and it would be foolish not to pursue competent instruction in it at some time. For that matter, the sport can also benefit anyone involved with medieval sword styles or even traditional Asian fighting arts. Although modern sport fencing may not be rapier dueling, this is not to say that exceptional fencers would not be excellent rapier fighters.

14. La Tousche developed a manner of using the rapier in two hands, but it never achieved any utility (for obvious reasons). Medieval estoc fighting, which used two hands, was much slower and a decidedly different fight. Books purporting to show a "two-handed" rapier are mistaken because these are only extended grips for greater reach.

15. This might explain the failure of many novice practitioners to understand the true nature of the rapier. They hold it incorrectly or still have a weak grip. As a result, from the start they feel more able to slash than thrust, despite the weapon's obvious design.

16. According to some sources, the term *pas d'âne* is incorrect and originally applied only to part of the cross-guard and only began to take on this meaning in the 18th century. Indeed, it likely refers to the double shell guard on later small-swords.

17. This, by the way, may help explain why a heavier, more substantially bladed sword does not really require such a compound guard: because its blade is capable of making blocks and solidly deflecting

15

cuts. It does not fight in-line and is not designed with thrust defense in mind. A heavier, compound hilt could even be a hindrance.

18.   Indeed, to facilitate touching angles, modern fencers are even known to put minute bends ('avantage) in their blades—something a real blade would never have had. It has occasionally been pointed out that several techniques of modern fencing, usable with light weapons and a set of rules, would not be nearly so possible with the historical weapons (particularly the manner of making whiplike "flicks" with the point). Rapier fighting was obviously far more brutal, and the combatants took great care in avoiding wounds. In contrast, sport fencers try to connect before the electric scorer registers their opponent's slower touch. This is a far cry from real duels, where combatants might slay each other and where even a wounded man might continue to strike back.

19.   As interesting as the history of personal duels is, this work is not concerned with them, but with a much wider approach to Renaissance sword use. The idea of single combat has always existed in Europe in some form: Greek champions issuing challenges, Roman gladiators, knights at tournament, and judicial duels (trial by combat). But the concept of the aristocratic "duel of personal honor" as practiced in the Renaissance and later years comes down from Germanic custom. It is worth noting that there are accounts of duels ending after the first blood had been drawn to "satisfy honor" (sometimes after the merest scratch). In others, the participants continued on aggressively even after suffering numerous stabs and cuts, both superficial and mortal.

20.   There is evidence that a certain degree of mystique arose around teachers and their methods, special moves, and secret techniques. Interestingly, geometry and mathematics seem to have been used occasionally to mystify rapier swordplay in a manner similar to the way Asian fighting arts often describe technique through use of Zen and Taoism.

21.   Occasionally, one hears of *kenjutsu* practitioners claiming that they'd "simply cut the rapier" in a fight. This is an astounding statement to make, considering not only the rapier's generally unfamiliar form and style, but also that cutting even a wooden weapon is difficult enough, let alone another metal blade that is moving even faster than their own. Seeing it in a movie doesn't make it real.

22.   It is interesting to note that the techniques of

Filipino stickfighting owes much of its development to the influence of Spanish explorers who colonized the islands. The Spaniards' rapier-and-dagger method of fighting must have been overwhelming (not to mention their firearms and cut-and-thrust blades). The influence of their two-weapon "fencing" style can be seen in the arts of *kali*, *arnis*, and *escrima*, which use short sticks and knives in place of historical machete-like blades (confiscated by the Spanish conquerors). Setting cultural pride aside, we should recognize that the rapier's techniques were judged valuable enough by the inhabitants to be incorporated into the native form. One wonders how then devotees of these martial arts can seemingly at once admit to the rapier's influence, but then indirectly dismiss its method as "inconsequential." Surprisingly, the modern Filipino stickfighting techniques involve little thrusting. Considering the historical precedent, one cannot help but speculate about the present potential of these arts against a skilled fencer or rapier fighter.

23.   As with any weapon that fosters a "style," use will favor certain muscle groups. This in turn, means the style will favor individuals whose physical makeup is more predisposed to doing so. Thus, some people do better in fencing combat or with a rapier than with other sword forms and vice versa. It is understandable that persons naturally taller, leaner, or smaller and more agile would take to the rapier more so than others (just as in the modern sport version). The ability to kill a larger, stronger opponent with a simple yet technically precise thrust was significant and psychologically intimidating.

24.   This is contrary to much of what passes for "historical re-creation" among many role-playing/fantasy organizations. This is made abundantly clear by the often idiotic stances and guards the enthusiasts in these organizations habitually attempt. Many of them usually lack even the rudiments of footwork and mobility. This phenomenon appears to come from not just lack of instruction, but misinterpretation of period drawings (many referring to cut-and-thrust swords). These will often make no tactical or technical sense unless one understands classical fencing, let alone practical cut-and-thrust swordplay, in the first place.

CHAPTER TWO

The Small-Sword

The small-sword is occasionally confused with the rapier. Although not precisely Renaissance swords, small-swords are an obscure area of weaponry that is often dismissed or ignored. Sometimes known as a "court sword," "walking sword," or "town-sword," this sword was even less suitable for war and more of a personal dueling tool than the rapier. Often said to have originated or been refined in France, the short sword was simply a weapon of self-defense. Despite belief by some that it was not a true sword, for the conditions under which it was required to perform, it was a fairly nasty little tool. With their smaller hilts and shorter lengths, the weapons also caused much less of a problem than rapiers when worn on crowded urban streets. Thus, they were dubbed "town-swords." In the late 1600s, the English began referring to these town-swords as "small-swords" (hence the name) as opposed to their own larger blades.

From the late 1600s to the late 1700s and early 1800s, the small-sword found favor with the upper classes. There were a great variety of small-swords, and many of them barely qualified as weapons. Many were best

known for their esthetic qualities. Highly decorated versions became fashionable as accessories, like jewelry, and were sometimes referred to as "costume swords." Of course, there was a difference between those small-swords that were actual weapons and those intended only as ornament for formal dress.

Although similar to their ancestor rapiers, small-swords had smaller guards and different blade shapes (cross-sections), ranging from rapierlike to hexagonal to diamond to rhomboid and triangular. Flat blade shapes were typical. Their blades also had some variation. At first, simply shorter, lighter forms of rapier blades were used. Later, much lighter diamond-shaped and then hollow-ground V-shaped blades, stronger and stiffer for thrusting were favored (the *colichemarde* or *Königsmarke* blade, wide near the hilt for parrying and then abruptly tapering). Because of its lightness and strength, the *colichemarde* supposedly enabled more techniques similar to those that would become common in sport fencing (sometimes, any triangular-shaped blade is referred to as a *colichemarde*). The small-sword consisted almost exclusively of a sharp-pointed metal rod and was hardly an edged weapon. The vast majority had no edge at all, being little more than pointed metal sticks—although some must have been sharpened because accounts of duels describe cuts "to the hands of the participants from grabbing."

Because their blades were also shorter and lighter, short swords were even faster in use than rapiers. In counteractions against thrusts, such potential agility allowed full use of parry and riposte techniques in a fight (block and counterattack in one motion). Disarms and moves to grab the opponent's wrist or weapon were also commonly taught. Attacks to the hand and forearm were especially common. small-swords could be easily held in what would be considered the French grip in modern fencing. The earlier complex guards and cup hilts of the rapier were changed into simple dish hilts or just ring guards. These guards were smaller and lighter because they were no longer necessary for protection against hits by heavier blades. A popular French method was developed that did not use "fingering" the ricasso. As a result, hilt branches and side rings on small-swords became obsolete. The second hand was also used less frequently because the small-sword was often too quick to grab. However, disarm techniques became more possible due to the minimal edge many possessed.

Many *salles d'armes* (schools of fence) sprang up throughout Europe in the 1700s. Eventually, small-sword movements were simplified and streamlined from those of rapiers by French masters. Many of the French masters wrote illustrated manuals defining and perfecting its use that have formed the basis of most modern fencing today. Footwork, parries, and counterthrusts were relied on for primary actions. Less emphasis was placed on the use of evasive motions, a second weapon, or the free hand. Names were also given to the directions of the various thrusts.

Manuscripts on small-sword use began to proliferate, including La Touche's in 1670, La Perche's in 1676, Sir William Hope's many works, André Liancour's in 1686, Labat's in 1690, Donald McBane's *The Expert Sword-Man's Companion* in 1728, Girard's in 1730, and Domenico Angelo's *The Schoole of Fencing* in 1763, Danet's in 1767, and numerous others into the 1800s.

Originally, small-swords were used against lighter rapiers, but in later periods they were even used to fight against cutting swords (spadroons, broadswords, hangers, etc.). Fighting with a small-sword and dagger or two small-swords was also known.

The small-sword, it should be remembered, existed under quite different circumstances than the rapier. It never really did have to face as effective cutting weapons as the rapier did in its day. Hence, it had even less reason for a heavier hilt and blade than the rapier did. Also, fighters in the age of the small-sword were themselves not nearly as skilled or experienced in cutting techniques as they had been in previous centuries. Never having had to fight daggers, bucklers, or two-swords, the small-sword was left free to develop may of the refined techniques associated with sport fencing today.

When witnessing the impressive reach and precision point control of modern fencing athletes, it is no wonder that a lighter thrusting weapon such as the small-sword became popular for dueling. Although this sword is perhaps lacking in defensive capability, it makes up for that with the lethality of its quick, penetrating, and graceful stabs (clear to anyone who has ever successfully used a fencing foil in sparring against a medieval or Asian sword). However, learning the offense with a thrusting sword—although a challenge—is not nearly as hard as learning to defend while point-on. The small-sword offers little protection or defense except against another small-sword or dagger.

Small-sword theory became quite advanced. It was not as brutal as fighting with rapiers and led more directly to modern sport fencing. Although more formidable, small-sword fighting closely resembles that of its descendants, the fencing foil and épée. Its stance and method of use doubtless involved very similar, if not identical, movements. In fact, a good deal of modern sport fencing's foundations originated with the dueling conventions of aristocracy and its emphasis on grace and poise (under such famous instructors as Dominico Angelo).

The users of small-swords developed their own etiquette and a formalized, elegant manner of use, but certainly not all duelists bothered with such contrived notions. It is likely that duelists still resorted to an "anything goes" approach when the time came. Interestingly, unlike those with rapiers, duels with small-swords seem to have ended more often after one party had sustained only a light injury. As 19th-century small-sword fencing grew into the familiar form we know today, there were a number of protocols and proprieties that were a direct result of practice without masks. With no safety headgear at the time, fencers had to be extremely careful not to injure their partners. Causing a face hit or injury was a serious error and major disgrace. Thus, an emphasis was placed on refined form and proper etiquette that went beyond what was necessary for any efficient physical mechanics. These elements survive today in some of sport fencing's customs and style. It also further distinguishes the nature of both small-sword and sport fencing from that of the rapier. As a sort of "junior rapier," the simple small-sword became the gentleman's weapon of choice in duels of honor during an age when the sword was well past its prime as a weapon of war and an exclusively thrusting style of swordsmanship had become a form all its own.

CHAPTER THREE

Cut-and-Thrust Swords

The Renaissance cut-and-thrust sword is somewhat ambiguous, with no real definition or precise identity. Furthermore, there is often confusion about the distinction between cut-and-thrust and rapier techniques, which is either misconstrued or ignored outright by many who currently practice various forms of swordplay.[1] Perhaps this is because so few individuals practice cut-and-thrust Renaissance swordsmanship; most seem to prefer a chivalric style of medieval warfare, romantic fencing, or samurai *budo*. The wide range of inaccurate replicas and medieval-fantasy swords available also adds to the confusion. The term *cut and thrust* is very general and can be applied to a whole range of sword forms. Indeed, the term is often applied by museum curators and collectors to almost any edged sword. At the time of the Renaissance, they were just referred to in the generic as "swords." In a sense, cut-and-thrust weapons are what swords are really all about.[2]

Rapiers themselves can be better understood by a study of the cut-and-thrust swords, which were both the rapiers' predecessors and contemporaries. This study will eliminate a good deal of the confusion that exists between the two. Renaissance fencing—or, rather, rapier fighting—should not be interpreted exclusively through the prism of modern fencing analysis. Useful as this may be, it is distorting. Rather, it should be viewed from the historical perspective of the earlier cut-and-thrust form. It is true that there are some references in the late 1400s and early 1500s that label what are clearly cut-and-thrust swords as rapiers, but this is because the term rapier had not yet taken on the meaning of a thrusting sword (the true rapier). The differentiation came about through a gradual process, just as it was to happen later for what was to become the small-sword. It is not just that some rapiers had cutting blades and others did not.

During the early 1500s, a distinction arose between swords intended for use on

21

battlefields and those for dueling and personal defense. The rapier's introduction into this caused controversy, particularly in England.

Swords for war naturally demanded a sturdy cutting and thrusting blade. Ideal swords at this time combined slashing and cutting potential with thrusting ability. They were sturdy for defense, but light and quick (crucial qualities in any weapon, but especially in a sword). The cut-and-thrust sword is a direct descendant of the medieval knightly sword. In Europe, they became the weapon of choice for battle and war during the Renaissance. They were used predominantly by foot soldiers, and it was not uncommon that a secondary weapon such a shield, buckler, or dagger (typically having substantial blades and sizable guards for parrying) was used. These weapons and their style of use were the precursors of the rapier and its "fencing" techniques.

The much mistaken and often ignored cut-and-thrust "Elizabethan" style of swordplay most assuredly relied on basic hack-and-slash moves such as those used with medieval swords. Users of these swords began to emphasize the one-handed quick stab to kill, which in turn necessitated more linear moves and tighter defense.[3] There is also good reason to believe that cut-and-thrust swordsmanship used more mobile footwork than in the earlier medieval form.[4] Being more mobile allowed fighters to make greater use of draw-cuts and close slashes (against unarmored opponents).

What happened was that fighters began to use their swords differently and their methods began to change. At the very least, they were certainly more careful about getting stabbed by a thrust. This change in style is reflected in many of the Elizabethan era illustrations in which figures are clearly not using the old hack-and-slash, sword-raised method. Instead, their weapons are usually

directed with the point toward the opponent. What we see is neither the medieval sword-and-shield, mass-combat style nor what we would think of as rapier fencing. Instead, the transitional style of the cut-and-thrust sword can be detected. The swords shown range from ones that look almost like rapiers to ones that appear medieval except for their guards.

It is this transitional style of the cut-and-thrust sword that causes so much confusion among sword enthusiasts who are trying to learn the craft and develop their techniques. We can only assume from these many illustrations that fighters of the time were not only exploring new forms of swords and new methods of employing their older weapons, but also systematizing what they already knew. It is with these cut-and-thrust swords that we begin to see the first signs of swordsmanship in Europe becoming more distilled and polished.

It is known that there were schools or associations in both France and Germany that adopted the rapier for defense (as practiced in Italian and Spanish schools) over the older cut-and-thrust method. It can be assumed that some form of continued practice with cut-and-thrust swords must have continued. But for the battlefield, the sword itself was becoming less and less relevant for the average warrior/foot soldier.

As has been well documented in the history of swords, lighter blades emerged as heavy armor use declined.[5] For many reasons, the lighter blades became increasingly common for civilian wear. The more that sword use focused on the thrust over the cut and the use of point-on stances, the more the sword grip became enclosed to protect the hand (this peaked with rapiers). This is easily apparent, but is often overlooked and understated. The swords from the "age of plate," during the late medieval period, reveal the origins of the transition to the cut-and-thrust forms.

With their narrower blades, stronger cross-sections, and tapered tips for thrusting into armor openings, we see in them something of the change toward a different form of swordsmanship. Ironically, the later cut-and-thrust variety of swords did not have to face the heavy armor that compelled the initial change in their medieval forerunners. Because of the advent of firearms and other weapons, these swords had to be used against only lightly or completely unarmored foes. This is a well-known but very significant development.

Some cut-and-thrust swords are indistinguishable from certain types of medieval blades, with the exception of incorporating the close or compound hilt (the "complex guard," i.e., extra quillons from the guard to pommel, sometimes known as counterbars or swept branches).[6] Some of their hilts had side rings or S-shaped side guards that increased protection to the fingers, the thumb, or the back of the hand. It is generally understood that among the first changes was the addition of round side sections or ring guards, sometimes incorrectly referred to as thumb rings (a bit of a misnomer since thumbs do not enter them and they can be on either side). The beginnings of finger loops (*pas d'âne*) can also be seen in them. There was no standard form of guard, but variations on the compound-hilt theme that changed with fashion over time. Without the wearing of armored gloves or gauntlets, increased hilt protection made sense. Enclosed guards, particularly knuckle bars, cage or basket hilts, and bell cups also offer the advantage of additional offense in that when close in, they can be used to punch and strike.[7]

What has been said about the development of compound hilts on Renaissance swords has so far been limited to the general suggestion that as armored gauntlets became less common, sword guards improved to make up for them. This is partially correct, but incomplete and overlooks the obvious. Before the use of gauntlets, many warriors using simple cross-guard hilts apparently did so without use of any gauntlets or hand armor. Saxon, Viking, and Frankish warriors are known to have rarely even used mail mittens, for example. To suggest that the compound hilt came about because hand armor had suddenly become impractical and unfashionable on the battlefield or for urban swordsmen is insufficient. As well, it has been established that as the technique of fingering the ricasso became more common in order to better use a sword's point, greater hand protection was required. This is because, as the sword was held less and less vertical and more and more horizontal, the grip was exposed both to thrusting attacks *and* cuts. It seems the exposure was due far more to the newer manner of sword use than to any lack of armored gloves.

There is then a major and obvious factor that appears to have been overlooked so far in describing the need for why the compound hilt developed. As cut-and-thrust forms of swords became more agile, they began to take advantage of directly meeting and engaging an opponent's own blade. By using the blade for blocking prior to counterattacking, a separation of movement into distinct actions of parry and riposte began. This can naturally be best managed only when one's sword is held more point-on (which didn't fully evolve until the rapier and later small-sword). This, of course, places the hand and grip in the path of oncoming blows *far more so* than when a sword is held more vertically in the familiar "medieval style" (or as in *kenjutsu*). Doing so can cause more and more hits to be taken on the hand. Thus, it then seems that this *increased use of in-line blade-play* (e.g., deflecting, blocking, beating, binding) was the major factor in developing a more enclosed and protecting hilt guard. The compound guard did not evolve just because fighters were being stabbed in the hand. This is particularly true of early rapiers facing cutting blades.

There is no doubt that because of their often similar hilts, cut-and-thrust swords are sometimes mislabeled as rapiers. As with some late medieval swords, cut-and-thrust swords can be found with extensive ricassos for use in fingering (which eventually lead to the newer method of gripping the rapier). In many later medieval swords and two-handed blades, a longer, extended ricasso acted as a "false grip." This allowed the second hand to grab the blade, thereby both adding power and increasing control for certain stabs. A few inches of thickened, often squared section of blade just above the hilt allowed for the long weapon to be shortened to improve its agility and handling when close in—not uncommon on larger swords, and maybe also aiding in hefting their weight. It may as well have added strength to that portion of the sword that received great stress. There was little need for that portion of the blade to be sharp anyway, because no cutting is done from there and it often clashes with the enemy's blade in close fighting. The ricasso evolved to allow for fingering and was developed fully in the late 1500s, but was occasionally found on late medieval swords.

Cut-and-thrust blades tended to be more slender and tapered, thus allowing for greater tip work and refined movements than did the relatively more brutal hack-and-slash medieval "style." In handling them, one can feel that most cut-and-thrust swords are still too awkward to be used in an exclusively thrusting, rapier-like manner (particularly with the many crude, poorly balanced imitation ones available). In a

way, the techniques can be said to resemble more those of modern saber fencing (from whence the sport must indirectly derive in at least some of its movements).

The pommels of some of these swords also showed changes. In addition to simple differences in style and ornamentation, pommels began to take on longer, more oval shapes. This tendency may have had to do with the alteration in handling that came about as the sword came to be used for greater thrusting. Such pommel shapes would certainly be more comfortable and less of a hindrance than the larger, flat ones required for counterbalance on heavier cutting swords—and may have aided late medieval sword use, such as when grabbing the pommel with the second hand to deliver stronger cuts.

By the mid-1500s, wearing swords with civilian dress became more acceptable and popular. Well-off commoners could now both carry and afford them. The demise of feudalism and the establishment of larger armies of common soldiers brought about a dramatic reduction in the opportunity for battlefield prestige by the individual warrior. The popularity of civilian dueling was in part a response to this. With the rise of crowded urban centers, it is no wonder that men took to settling their disputes by streetfights and duels instead of the more traditional tournaments and trial by combat. Thus, a method of personal sword-and-dagger fighting began to appear. This eventually supplanted the sword-and-buckler method. Being more common and easier to carry, daggers were found to be naturally more offensive.

The versatility of a cut-and-thrust blade was that in a skilled hand (singular) it could often be used to outfight the more "traditional" medieval sword under the new conditions emerging in warfare (i.e., pike, musket, cannon). Not having to be used to penetrate battlefield armor, cut-and-thrust blades were by nature somewhat lighter and thus more maneuverable. A few quick, simple, but well-placed cuts could often decide a fight before any devastating hack or slash could be delivered.[8] Later on, though, these swords could not usually be used to outmaneuver the thrusting rapier in *single* combat. This was not so much a matter of a superior weapon as of well-executed mechanics: the more skillful swordsman, not the weapon, invariably wins. It is likely that no early rapier fighter was entirely without skill or knowledge in the use of cut-and-thrust swords, and there was undoubtedly a substantial crossover of technique.

Perhaps, one could speculate that the ascendancy of thrusting over cutting came about as sword fights in the "civilized" areas of town and city became more common than the chaotic clash of arms and men on the battlefield. When on foot on the medieval battlefield, one charged an armored opponent and hacked away, whereas the new Renaissance methods of warfare focused on ranged attacks and close-order drill. There was arguably less opportunity and reason to cross swords man-to-man in the heat of battle. In contrast, fighting off the battlefield was more often than not preceded by an interval that probably allowed the participants to draw their weapons, face off, and make the conscious decision to engage. Excluding the likely incidents of ambush and surprise backstab, fighting this way certainly encouraged the investigation and practice of different uses of the sword.

Off the battlefield and without armor, learning how to move more carefully and use a weapon for self-defense took somewhat different tactics. Shields had also become less relevant and convenient for swordsmen at the time (not to mention

impractical and unfashionable for civilian dress). Therefore, it is reasonable to conceive that a method came about through experiences in duels, brawls, and schools that gave preference to the swordsman who pointed his sword and quickly stabbed rather than the one who raised it for a slash or vicious cut. Eventually, swordsmen must have started taking up positions at the onset of a fight in which the sword was immediately pointed at the opponent. This allowed both combatants to ward off and threaten at the start of a fight without having to make a cut or take a swing. Once this obvious concept became commonplace among the crowded, restless urban populace, it was inevitable that swords designed more suitably for this would be produced.

The more a weapon allows the performance of a particularly useful move or technique, the more that move or technique will be used. The more the move is used, the better one becomes at it and the more one will tend to select a weapon that permits and encourages such technique. As with most weapons, this is the dynamic at work with swords and explains much of their development (especially in the case of cut-and-thrust swords and the rapier). All this may be somewhat obvious, but it needs to be restated. Whatever one's natural inclinations, when facing opponents without heavy armor, one's sword choice will naturally favor a quicker, more agile weapon, as long as it is sturdy.[9]

That the value of cutting was deeply held can perhaps be better understood by using boxing as an analogy. Many people who may have never studied the mechanics of boxing or even been in fights will still instinctively know that throwing a powerful punch can be very effective. With boxing training, a fighter learns the effectiveness of bobbing and weaving while throwing straight jabs. Boxing teaches methods to counter and outfight the natural and more powerful "roundhouse" punch. The same approach was used by advocates of the early thrusting blades against those wielding traditional cut-and-thrust swords. The historical issue of "cut vs. thrust," or whether a sword's focus should be on use of the edge or point, is really not as important as is sometimes claimed (particularly by sport fencers today). Cutting with a blade is an extremely effective and lethal thing to do. It has always been very useful, else so many types of cutting swords would not have come to exist. It is only when we look at single combat without armor that the advantages (but not complete superiority) of thrusting weapons become apparent. This is precisely what happened in the centuries following the Middle Ages.

At the time, feudalism was fading. There was a rising, urban middle class who could not only afford swords (which were also being made better), but could go around wearing them. There was an end to the social structure that gave an outlet to hostilities at the same time that individual prowess on the battlefield was becoming less and less relevant. The result of all this was a proliferation of dueling. This in turn had the natural effect of turning individuals to a serious, scientific pursuit of the techniques of personal swordsmanship.

Thus, we come to the question of how do we tell which Renaissance blades are thrusting rapiers and which are for cutting? This is the same question that Renaissance swordsmen of the age faced. We can answer it the same way they undoubtedly did. To settle any confusion once and for all over which Renaissance blades are true rapiers and which are cutting swords, it is only necessary to do three simple things. (1) Take an *accurate* reproduction rapier and spend a day trying to sharpen a cutting edge on it. (2) Take an accurate, *unsharpened* replica of

a cut-and-thrust sword, place a safety tip on it, and then try to "fence." You can't do it. The weapon is not nearly agile enough for the usual disengages, coupes, and ripostes. (3) Take an accurate, *fully* sharpened cut-and-thrust blade and spend a week with it cutting at thick card-board tubes. You will soon see that simple flicks of the wrists for drawing slices using six or eight inches of blade, or even chops from the elbow, are all quite insufficient for effective cutting. Cutting properly is not that easy. Considering how few historical blades fall in between either the cutting form or the true rapier, it would seem that the answer to the question of what kind of blade could do what had been settled. The evolution of this is clear in the period fighting manuals. Despite the well-reasoned effectiveness of the Renaissance cut-and-thrust sword, for personal urban self-defense and dueling, the thin, *thrusting* rapier became dominant.

There were also a variety of shorter, broader, enclosed-hilt military swords used (primarily by cavalry) in the 1600s. Many were given names by 19th-century collectors (such as the walloon, sinclair, or mortuary) and classed as backswords or broadswords. There was also the Italian *schiavona* closed cage or basket-hilt sword (named after hired soldiers or *sciavonni*). Forerunner of the Scottish claymore, the *schiavona* saw limited use. Often during the Renaissance, many older style blades were also fitted with newer style hilts. Our focus here is not on these swords (most of which did not have ricassos or involve fingering), but on the earlier form of which the rapier is related.

The forms of swords used were not only a product of the armor faced or the opponents confronted, but also of personal, societal, and cultural choices (e.g., physical build, metallurgy, weight, cost). Furthermore, style, or rather fashion, was an element that cannot be overlooked. This was very much the case with both cut-and-thrust swords and the rapier.

As the rapier developed, spread, and declined over a period of roughly 200 years (circa 1500–1700), other cut-and-thrust sword forms were still in favor. Being too useful in war, however, they never completely disappeared; they always survived in some form, particularly later as spadroons, hangers, dusaks, cutlasses, and sabers (this is understandable, considering the rapier's own unsuitability on horseback, which, again, is due to its limited cutting power).

Just as medieval swords had given way, the cut-and-thrust variety, through practicality and necessity, began to be displaced in personal combat by the increasingly popular rapiers. To properly understand and practice with either cut-and-thrust swords or rapiers, the distinction between the two must be recognized.

NOTES

1. The difference between medieval sword use and cut-and-thrust use is sometimes not all that clear either. Numerous medieval swords are equally capable of stabbing as well as cutting.
2. In fact, many swords of the world fall into the cut-and-thrust category, including curved blades that are designed primarily to slash or draw-cut. Many short swords, used for stabbing, can also be employed for delivering cuts.
3. In the Middle East, India, and Indonesia, a somewhat more circular and flowing style emerged for similar reasons.
4. Although forms of cut-and-thrust swords were used on horseback, it was on foot that the change in the nature of sword use took place. Single-edged variations also became popular with the newer, lighter mounted troops, since the deeper angle allowed for a better cut while riding.
5. At the height of the "age of plate," certain thrusting weapons of heavy, stiff, square- or diamond-shaped "blades" were devised specifically for jamming into

and piercing the gaps and joints of heavy armor. Although they clearly were not used in the same manner as cut-and-thrust swords or rapiers, it is interesting to speculate what influence weapons such as the English and German *tuck* and French *estoc* and Italian *stocco* may have had on rapier development. Occasionally, rapiers with triangular or squarish blades are incorrectly called tucks, although (as Arthur Norman points out in *The Rapier and Small-Sword 1460–1820*) no period literature ever referred to the weapon as such and even made distinctions between them.
6. The main crossbars of sword guards are often called *quillons*, a term applying to Renaissance swords, not medieval swords.
7. The word *pummel* comes from *pommeling* or hitting with the sword pommel.
8. Eventually, all this was to lead to the rapier, then the small-sword, and finally the sport of fencing in the last century (some techniques of which are actually quite recent innovations).
9. The argument sometimes heard that rapiers could draw-cut strongly or slice through bone because there also existed a rare "sword-rapier" form is self-defeating. If rapiers could cut anyway, why have another sword-rapier form at all?

Obviously, the rapier's deficiency in cutting and the cut-and-thrust sword's slower speed and agility in stabbing were the motivations behind the few attempts to produce so-called sword-rapiers. It is unlikely that these uncommon swords were merely transition forms between the cut-and-thrust variety and the rapier. It is more probable that they were an attempt to make either a cut-and-thrust blade that could stab as quickly as the new rapier or a rapier that could still slice like the older cut-and-thrust form. There is no real evidence either way.

Practitioners who handle their rapiers, *schlagers*, or épées in the manner of a true rapier cannot just arbitrarily throw in a few draw-cuts now and then and excuse the practice by making some vague reference to a sword-rapier. In doing so, they are missing the point (figuratively and literally). In sparring, a person must decide whether he is simulating a rapier or a sword-rapier. It can't be both. If the person claims that he's simulating some form of sword-rapier, then he should be forced to validate this claim by demonstrating the sword's slower speed and handling. After all, the advantage of a cutting edge on a blade comes at the price of increased weight and width—which means less agility, speed, and length (three crucial elements of a thrusting sword).

Weapons and Their Use

RAPIER

Rapiers differed in overall length somewhat, ranging from 42 to 48 inches. Blade lengths were approximately 36 to 40 inches, although even longer ones were known. Weight varied as the weapon changed, preferences evolved, and users began favoring different ones they could handle better. (Rapier is pronounced more accurately "ray-peer," rather than "raypee-er.")

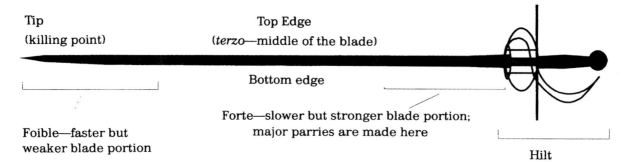

Tip
(killing point)

Top Edge
(*terzo*—middle of the blade)

Bottom edge

Forte—slower but stronger blade portion;
major parries are made here

Foible—faster but
weaker blade portion

Hilt

Example of "Basic" Swept Hilt

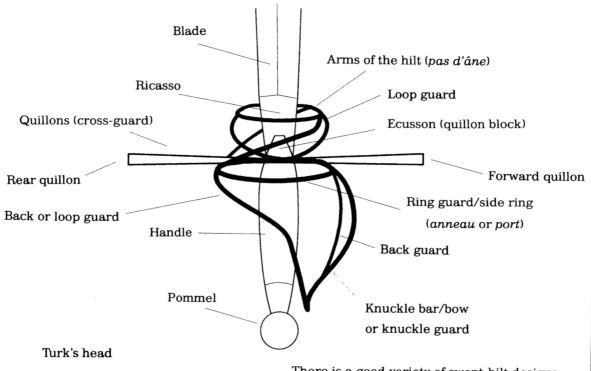

Blade

Arms of the hilt (*pas d'âne*)

Ricasso

Loop guard

Quillons (cross-guard)

Ecusson (quillon block)

Rear quillon

Forward quillon

Back or loop guard

Ring guard/side ring
(*anneau* or *port*)

Handle

Back guard

Pommel

Knuckle bar/bow
or knuckle guard

Turk's head

Tang button
or pommel nut

There is a good variety of swept-hilt designs, from simple curved guards to enclosing cage and basket hilts, but they all follow particular patterns based on utility (i.e., weight, balance, comfort, protection). The compound guard actually developed first with the cut-and-thrust sword. Similar, even identical, swept-hilt forms were used for both Renaissance swords and rapiers, which is a major reason for some of the confusion between the two. The great variety of hilts was a result of fashion and regional differences.

EXAMPLES OF BLADES

As with later small swords, there is some question about which rapiers were for actual use by fighters and which were for decoration only. There is no doubt, from the great number of blade types, that swordsmanship throughout the Renaissance was a matter of earnest investigation.

Early rapier. Note width of blade.

Typical swept hilt. Note wider forte.

Typical cage hilt. Note the squarish shape at the forte.

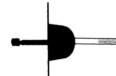

Cup hilt with "ideal" rapier blade. Note the length and width.

Dish hilt type or cavalier, transition type, with shorter blade, wider at forte.

Typical early small sword.

Example of *colichemarde*-style small sword.

Modern fencing épée.

Modern fencing foil.

RAPIER BLADES

These side-section views of a typical rapier blade reveal their diamond-like shape. They could also be flat-hexagonal- or oval-shaped. Note the steep angle of the edges. Contrast this with the view of an average cut-and-thrust blade.

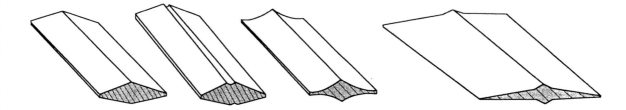

The blade cross-sections of an early form of small-sword blade and two types of average triangular small-sword blades compared with the modern fencing épée and fencing foil with its squarish shape. Below each is a view of the blade near its tip.

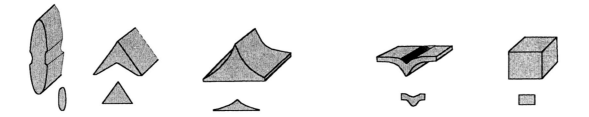

For training and sparring, practitioners today use a variety of weapon substitutes, including the following: sport fencing épées, extrawide theatrical or stage combat épées, historical replicas of varying quality, and even fiberglass rods. Probably the most popular for simulating rapiers are oval- or triangular-shaped *Schlager* blades (derived from obscure 16th-century German cutting swords later adapted as 19th-century *Mensur* student dueling weapons). Long *schlager* blades make good rapier simulators in that they are stiffer and heavier than sport fencing weapons. They, therefore, must be handled with more historical techniques and fewer of those of modern fencing. Accurate reproduction rapiers do not require the same safety flex of sport fencing weapons. They were meant, after all, to penetrate, not touch. They were also not meant for the endless banging and slashing of typical theatrical fights. The choice of which sword type to use seems to depend as much on affordability as the rules to be practiced under and the martial spirit of the users. Practicing with replicas of actual rapiers reveals just how differently they function than modern fencing versions and their cut-and-thrust relatives.

RAPIER POINTS

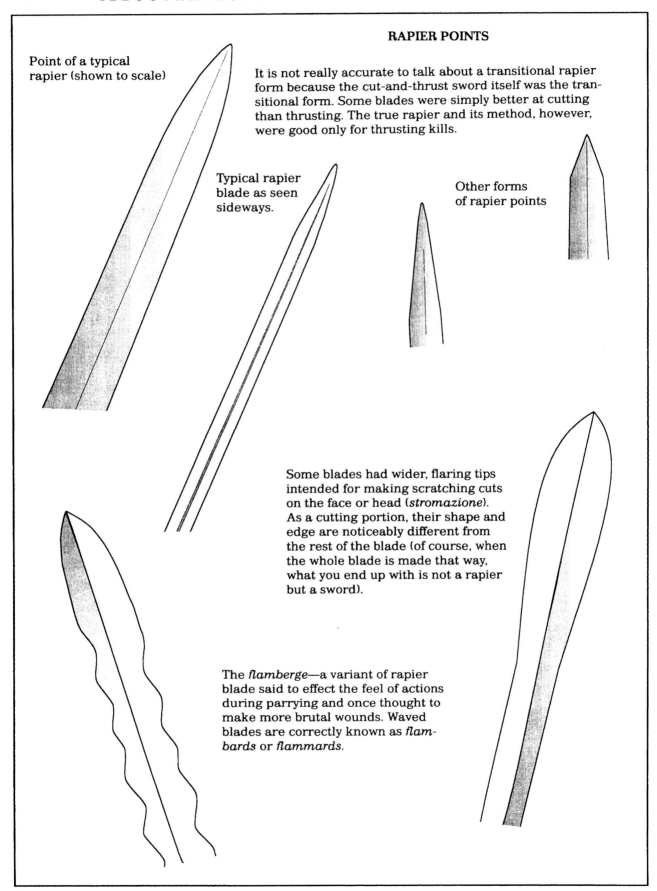

Point of a typical
rapier (shown to scale)

It is not really accurate to talk about a transitional rapier
form because the cut-and-thrust sword itself was the transitional form. Some blades were simply better at cutting
than thrusting. The true rapier and its method, however,
were good only for thrusting kills.

Typical rapier
blade as seen
sideways.

Other forms
of rapier points

Some blades had wider, flaring tips
intended for making scratching cuts
on the face or head (*stromazione*).
As a cutting portion, their shape and
edge are noticeably different from
the rest of the blade (of course, when
the whole blade is made that way,
what you end up with is not a rapier
but a sword).

The *flamberge*—a variant of rapier
blade said to effect the feel of actions
during parrying and once thought to
make more brutal wounds. Waved
blades are correctly known as *flam-
bards* or *flammards*.

EXAMPLES OF RAPIER BLADES AND RICASSO

Various examples of "typical" rapier blades and ricasso showing fullers, raised ridges, and tangs.

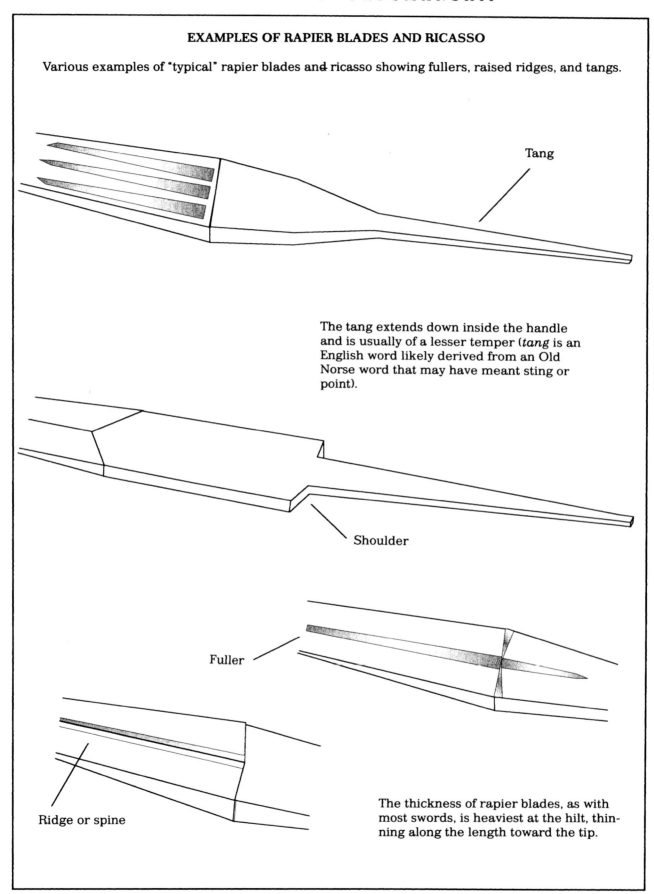

Tang

The tang extends down inside the handle and is usually of a lesser temper (*tang* is an English word likely derived from an Old Norse word that may have meant sting or point).

Shoulder

Fuller

Ridge or spine

The thickness of rapier blades, as with most swords, is heaviest at the hilt, thinning along the length toward the tip.

RAPIER HILTS

The average weight of rapiers varied considerably, especially with the type of hilt attached, but also with the blade length and shape. A rough estimate would be about 2.7 pounds. The hilt mountings (guard, handle, pommel, etc.) were often made detachable and, therefore, replaceable. The blade was made by one craftsman and the hilt by another, and often a third person would piece them together. Being civilian weapons, rapiers were often ornately decorated.

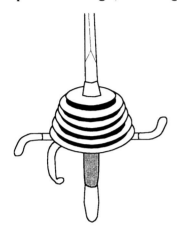

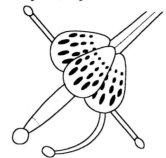

Hilt with "shell guard" plates and knuckle bar.

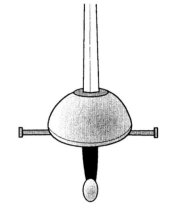

Typical "cage hilt" or "ring hilt." Developing from the swept hilt, it offered more protection and led to the shell and disc hilt forms. They might have from four to eight rings.

An example of a pierced-disc hilt.

The familiar Spanish cup hilt style did not appear until the 1650s. Once sword duels became predominately thrusting fights, cup hilts developed later as a natural progression of defense.

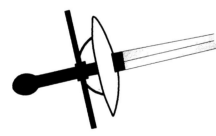

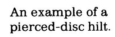

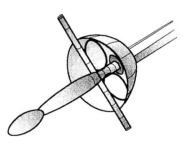

A "dish hilt"-style rapier, precursor to the later small sword. Starting only in the last century, some dish-hilt or "dueling hilt" rapiers began to also be called *flambergs* by scholars.

Example of "typical" cup hilt with quillons, ricasso, and *pas d'âne* inside. The French term *quillon* is likely derived from an older Latin term referring to reeds.

Hilts of typical small swords.

Colichemarde style.

TOOLS OF THE MODERN SPORT

Modern épée.

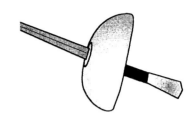

The triangular-bladed épée (French for sword) really has more in common with the small sword than the rapier, despite retaining the cup hilt. It developed in France in the late 1800s as a form of codified dueling weapon. It eventually evolved into its own sport that still retains some of this aspect. Early versions were stiffer and heavier than those today. Modern épées have the blade slightly off-center to allow more hand protection and safety tips instead of earlier blunted prongs. The rules for épée fencing resemble more those of the classic duel than either those of foil or saber fencing.

Total length is approximately 43 inches, weight is between 1 and 2 pounds, and cup guard is 5 inches wide. Blades of modern fencing weapons have been standardized to about 36 inches.

The modern French-grip foil (configured to fit the hand).

(3-to-4-inch-diameter disk guard)

The square-bladed foil developed as a practice weapon for the small sword in the late 1700s (possibly in Germany). The practice evolved into the gentlemanly art of fencing. It was later also used for épée practice. The foil is sometimes know as the *fleuret* (from the French *fleur*, flower) because either its covered tip resembled a flower bud or the earliest versions had hilts of two hollow, figure-eight, petal-like ring guards descended from those on small swords. Nineteenth-century sport fencing foils retained this guard and added leather pads. Later the traditional disk guard was used. The metal-mesh fencing mask was also developed in the late 1800s by the French master La Boksshire.

The term *foil* was first used in the 1630s and referred to various types of practice swords whose edges and tips were blunted or "foiled." The word comes from the French *fouler*, meaning to press or turn (back). Originally, foiling one's weapon meant to blunt or pad its tip (with cloth, leather, or wood). Historically, practice weapons were not uncommon and usually were just dulled, blunted versions of real ones. For rapier practice, tips were known to have been folded over or blunted and then sometimes wrapped with cloth or leather.

Italian-grip foil.

Modern fencing grips require that the weapon be easily released for safety. Thus, the Spanish grip (similar to the Italian) is illegal in competition.

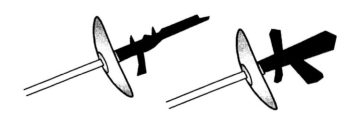

Two examples of the variety of unusual, modern anatomical fencing grip styles. The many branch-like protrusions help grip and point control.

GRIPPING THE RAPIER

A proper grip is fundamental, but holding the sword can be a matter of personal preference relative to both grip strength and style of use. There are various ways of gripping, often subject to the user's strength and dexterity, and the balance and reach desired. On a thrust, the edges may face either horizontally (which can aid in slipping it between the ribs) or vertically, depending on the hand position.

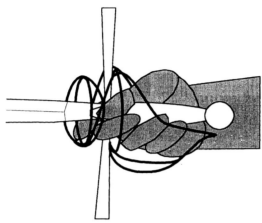

Note the forefinger looped around the ricasso and the second finger over the cross-guard. The thumb is also sometimes placed on the ricasso.

An exceptionally strong hand may even grip the weapon just from the handle and pommel. This can increase reach, but it also weakens action. Some hilts were ambidextrous, but most were designed for right hands.

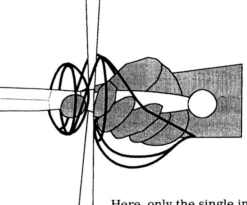

Here, only the single index finger is being used to grip.

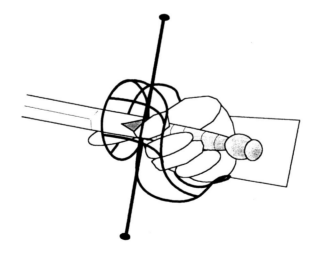

In this grip, notice the extended index finger for even more control and comfort. Some instructors advised against leaving it so exposed, lest it be injured or broken.

The material used for grips varied from leather to cloth or felt. Many were bound with wire. Grips of bone, ivory, or horn were popular. For comfort and protection, the ricasso was also sometimes covered in leather or velvet.

GRIPS

For control and angle-of-attack, gripping the weapon is usually managed "in pronation" (with the knuckles up), but it may also call for the knuckles to be held down ("supination"). It can also be held midway between the two in the more natural position of simply pointing the index finger.

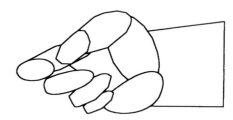

An example of the usual hand position for gripping the rapier. Note the similarities between this grip and the one for a cut-and-thrust blade (below).

The feel of a good rapier is subjective. However, it has been suggested that, for better handling, a point of balance about 3 inches from the top guard is best.

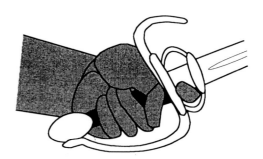

The standard traditional grip for both small sword (also the modern Italian grip) and modern fencing foil (French grip) is somewhat lighter than that for a rapier. Manipulation of the rapier involves more wrist and arm control than use of the hand and fingers, as in modern fencing.

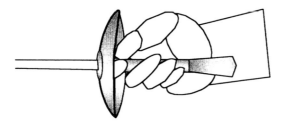

Modern foil.

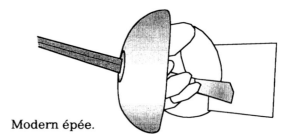

Modern épée.

TECHNIQUES

Note: It is nearly impossible to describe in words and pictures alone sufficient detail to instruct in technique or proper movement form. These examples are meant to be informative, not representative of all possibilities. They are general, not universal or definitive, fighting instructions. Here, only certain basic concepts and principles of rapier or cut-and-thrust fighting will be referred to. Much of the material will likely be unfamiliar to those without some rudimentary knowledge of fencing. All examples are shown from a right-handed perspective. Also, the majority of the terms that come down to us are of Italian or French origin. Recent scholarship and research have given us a fuller understanding of Renaissance swords and their use, even though in those days much of it was imprecise and not always consistent.

The typical rapier stance contrasted with
a modern fencing on-guard (*en garde*) position.

The basic stances are somewhat more offensive in nature than defensive or neutral, considering that the "business end" is immediately aimed and threatening from the start (understandable when using a *thrusting* or "foining" weapon).

STANCE

Although there developed a basic, practical form of rapier ready stance or on-guard position, there will also be certain limited variations because of personal style. One uses what is effective and efficient—in other words, whatever works.

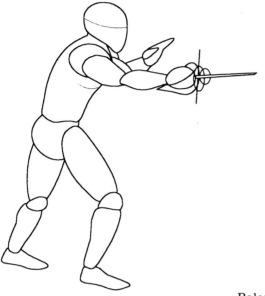

Stance is more forward, allowing the use of the second hand and either leg to lead. The posture is relatively straight with the back not leaning too far forward. Feet should be placed shoulder-width apart and evenly balanced.

Balance is evenly distributed. However, because the rear foot gives force to forward movement, more weight tends to be placed on it. At times, balance may be centered on the balls of the feet for mobility (as in boxing); at other times, it is concentrated in the heels.

The free arm is raised as a counterbalance and to keep it out of the way.

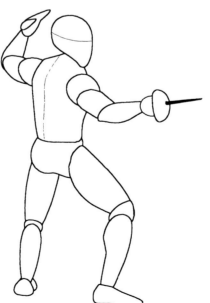

Shoulder is relaxed, and elbow is bent.

When advancing in the smooth, simultaneous foot-work of modern fencing, the toes lift first and then the heel. In retreating, the reverse is followed. The lead foot is always pointed toward the opponent.

Feet are placed at 90-degree angles, and knees are slightly bent.

The Italian Masters of Defence deduced roughly three basic rapier stances or *guardia: prima, seconda, terza*—roughly equivalent to a high-, middle-, and low-sword position.

Notice the varying positions the second hand can assume. Too close and it can be attacked; too far and it's ineffective. Ideally, it remains limber enough to grab or block. Although useful in defense, the hand could also be struck or pierced as part of a distracting or prepatory attack.

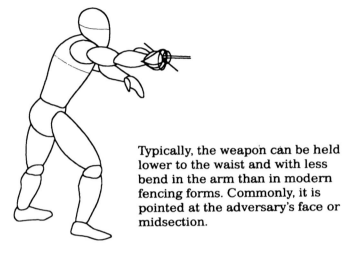

Typically, the weapon can be held lower to the waist and with less bend in the arm than in modern fencing forms. Commonly, it is pointed at the adversary's face or midsection.

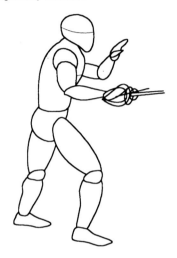

With the rapier, even more so than in modern fencing, in order to deliver quick, powerful stabs, it is necessary to keep the attacking arm straight. The arm cannot be too straight, or it will quickly tire. If bent too far, it lacks speed and reach, as well as exposing the forearm.

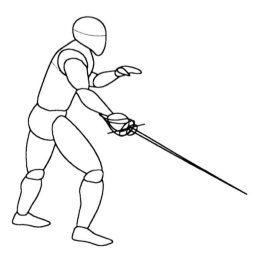

Here, the single sword (*spada solo*) is held in a form of low-guard position (or low ward), usually to act as an invitation for the opponent to attack. The second hand can be more to the right or the left.

Rapier stances naturally have much in common with those postures used with cut-and-thrust swords. Eventually, they evolved more distinctive stances based on the rapier's own dynamic. There was a good deal of stylistic difference in these that seems to have been of personal and national choice more than anything else.

Rapier footwork is not nearly the fluid, developed form used in fencing today, but a more natural one using a variety of steps and skipping hops. It can lead with either leg, depending on the need. However, in the act of maneuvering (advancing, retreating, traversing, voiding, etc.) there should be no extraneous movement or dancing about.

It goes without saying that from the very beginning proper balance (equally on both legs in an upright posture) is vitally important in using any techniques of swordsmanship. It is surprising how often this is violated by novices with poor posture or foot positioning.

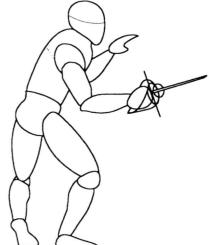

In addition to the stances and guards, it is evident in the footwork that rapier combat has a necessarily different flow and tempo than the cut-and-thrust sword form. It is also heavier and less elegant than modern fencing. Footwork can involve stepping forward with the lead foot first, hopping forward or back with both, advancing with the rear leg, or dropping back with the lead leg (cross-stepping). Sidestepping or "traversing" forward or back is also used. It is from this form of movement that evasions are made and power added to thrusts by pushing off the rear leg. As long as the proper mechanics are used and no motion wasted, there is considerable room for personal style when moving.

For individuals during the mid-1500s to early 1700s faced with life-threatening quarrels, duels of honor, or day-to-day chance encounters with sword-wielding attackers, the rapier provided a good means of self-protection. It also provided a new means of demonstrating martial prowess because many personal quarrels turned into excuses for group fights. Fundamentally, the weapon is about keeping an attacker at a distance—*and killing him there*. Its deadly point aimed at the opponent forces him to have to come closer and pass it at the risk of being punctured. It is interesting that a weapon, evolving from earlier cut-and-thrust swords, would progress to an almost entirely new method of swordsmanship or "fence" (*scherma* in Italian, *escrime* in French).

The standard lunge of modern fencing and an example of its equivalent with the rapier (known by such terms as *stocata lunga, affondo,* or *punta sopramano*). The second hand may be lowered behind to improve balance or left in place for defense. The first description of the equivalent movement of a lunge was the *lunga* of Nicoletto Giganti in the *Treatro* of 1606, and not Capo Ferro in 1610. Ferro established its significance with thrusting rapiers. The purpose of the lunge is to quickly extend the reach of a thrusting attack into an open target area. With a rapier, and especially a small sword, the lunge is a powerful and effective technique.

Although the techniques of modern competitive fencing are not accurate or entirely reproducible for rapier combat, they are nonetheless relevant and instructive. It is important to know both what is and what is not possible with a weapon. Sport fencing provides a firm place to start studying the rapier and leads to a certain degree of understanding. It is true that we can learn from looking at what the rapier turned into, but we must also look from where it came.

Generally, the weapon is moved *simultaneously* with any footwork. At other times the weapon may move first, followed almost immediately by stepping. A small step or movement of the foot may also be used in a feint (an *impetinata*).

To achieve maximum reach, the lead foot is generally that of the sword hand. This also allows better agility and reach.

More agile footwork also requires lighter footwear. Is it any wonder then that modern fencing relies on such light footwear or that Japanese fencing (*kendo*) uses none at all? In fact, a vast number of manuscripts, effigies, statues, and other works of art depicting foot gear of medieval and Renaissance warriors invariably show soft shoes with noticeably small heels.

Sidestepping outside with the rear leg (*quartata*) as a means of evasion or countermaneuver. A variation (the *volte*) extends the leg around and forward. A running attack or jump lunge may be made by the rear foot crossing in front of the lead (a *fleche* or arrow).

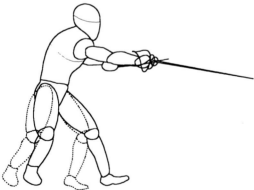

Leading with the left rear leg can close the distance to an opponent, but also lessen the reach of the rapier. It can also be deceptive and allow for better use of the free hand or dagger.

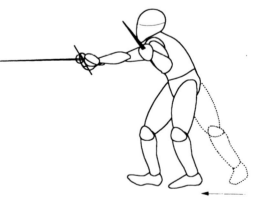

For proper, even balance and efficiency of movement, the distance between the feet, about 1 to 2 feet is maintained when advancing, retreating, or traversing.

The nature of a thrusting weapon, such as the rapier, demands high mobility while extending the arm to stab or parry. It involves a great deal of shifting, feinting, probing, and waiting. Much of it can be a kind of tense stillness as each swordsman tries to judge the opponent's intentions and imminent actions and respond in a burst of movement. Perhaps more so than with earlier sword combat, rapiers have a rhythm more reminiscent of a boxing match. The combatants look for openings, warily throw a few jabs, and are ever ready to land a decisive blow. Calmness of mind is essential. Modern sport fencing has developed a similar feel to a high degree. It is this method that rapier enthusiasts attempt to investigate and re-create today. However, the thought is always present that, unlike in either boxing or sport fencing, "touches" with real rapiers could be lethal.

If sport fencing today is "a conversation in steel,"
then the rapier was an all-out argument.

Fighters of the time practiced with both real and blunted weapons against stationary targets and sparring partners (not always at full intensity for the latter, it can be assumed). But there was no substitute for the experience gleaned from actual encounters. In real fights, there were no rules, and you won at any cost.

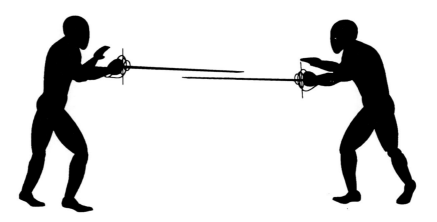

Engaging with rapiers in
appropriate fighting distance.

A rapier's length was a personal matter, depending on the fighting style of the user. For a brief time, very long rapiers were in favor. Although an advantage of a few inches in blade length can make a major difference, skilled fighters can learn to close in and tie up a much longer weapon.

Primary targets of choice include the face, abdomen, underarm, chest, and hand. Although simple thrusts to the face or gut can be very effective, those to the ribs or sternum that strike bone may not be so. Often, as the opponent moves, the back and buttocks become a target.

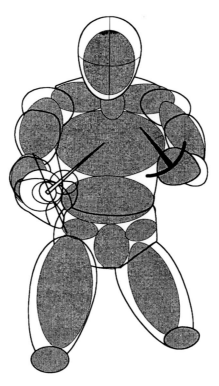

The rapier's primary targeting sites
for lethal or incapacitating thrusts.

With the obvious exception of the knee, the legs are not a prime target for the rapier for obvious reasons. Because thrusts there are unlikely to produce any wound that will either incapacitate or kill an opponent outright, there is little or no reason to attack there. Except as a distraction or effort to wear the adversary down, doing so would likely expose the fighter to greater peril (indeed, the classical masters make little or no reference to attacks there). Even a solid thrust through the hip or the meat of the thigh would likely expose the swordsman to greater peril. Striking the meat of the thigh would likely not prevent the adversary from counterstriking immediately. Using a rapier to cut arteries under the thick muscles of the inner thigh is also improbable, if not impossible. It is quite possible to receive substantial rapier stabs to the legs without the stab's preventing one from moving or standing. Nor would such a stab in the thigh or cut on the shinbone cause an individual to drop to the ground and remain in a sitting or kneeling position (voluntarily or involuntarily). However, a stab to the foot, always a possibility, could be a serious distraction. Historical accounts of duels support all this. Fencing is about mobility, which is to say *footwork*. As rapier, and later small-sword, fighters learned, movement is the very foundation of a thrusting weapon. Duels could not continue from such static positions without the standing party immediately finishing his opponent off. To believe otherwise is fantasy, and enthusiasts who practice under artificial rules construed to require this sort of thing are limiting themselves. Worse, they are wasting valuable training time because either they or their opponents sit around on the ground. Sadly, many practitioners hold mind-sets more focused (consciously or not) on the role playing and fantasy of swordsmanship than on the martial aspects of fighting skill.

In modern fencing, the four areas or lines have names that depend on whether the hand is held palm up (supination) or palm down (pronation). Up = *sixte, quarte, octave, septime*; down = *tierce, quinte, seconde, prime*. A thrust made to the adversary's inside targets was usually pronated; a thrust made outside was usually supinated.

An example of four major parrying areas. All attacks (and parries) fall into one of the four areas: inside, outside, high, or low. Unlike in modern fence, the center line cannot usually be directed at the opponent's weapon.

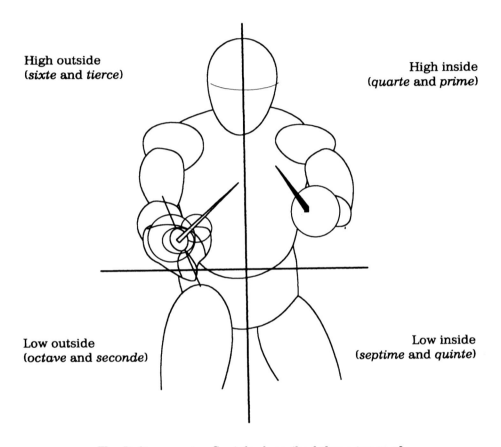

High outside
(*sixte* and *tierce*)

High inside
(*quarte* and *prime*)

Low outside
(*octave* and *seconde*)

Low inside
(*septime* and *quinte*)

The Italian master Saviolo described three types of thrusts as *imbroccata* (over the top of the adversary's sword), *stoccata* (under the adversary's sword or grip), and *punta reversa* (to the left or the outside of the sword). A straight thrust was also sometimes referred to as a *botta dritta*.

Keep in mind that rapier thrusting attacks do not have to travel in a straight line or with the blade horizontal. The tip can trace a deceptively circular or snaking path as it races to a target under, over, or around the adversary's grip. This angulation of stabbing attacks can be formidable. However, real rapiers are less maneuverable than their modern fencing counterparts, and thrusts with them sometimes require a slightly straighter angle to penetrate effectively. Unlike the relatively light, flicking taps and stabs of modern fencing, a rapier's attack needed much more of an exerted commitment to pierce the target. That is why people often speak of small-sword *play*, as opposed to rapier *fighting*.

FUNDAMENTAL DEFENSE AGAINST RAPIER THRUSTING ATTACKS

As fighters learned to parry with a sword point-on, there were perhaps originally eight basic parries used. They are really only the natural, instinctive moves that one would make to deflect a stabbing attack by moving the stronger part of the blade (the forte) against the attacker's weaker part (foible). In each, the need to maintain the tip pointed at the opponent is apparent. Eventually, the "true" parry, opening a line of thrusting attack as the block is made, was a significant change. It later became a primary feature of small-sword use.

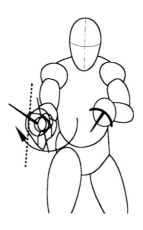

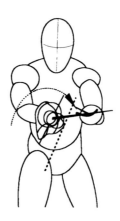

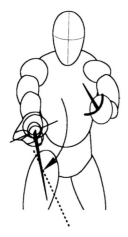

As with most sword forms, parries are made using the forte, the stronger portion of the blade nearest the hilt. Parries with the rapier differ from those with cut-and-thrust swords in that rather than having to move the whole blade, they can be made with more of a turn or rotation of the grip or hilt. There are a few variations of style that exist for this.

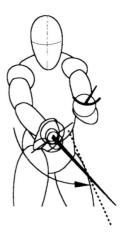

To use the blade's right side (true edge) in blocking or opposing, a parry made inside was usually supinated, and the one outside was usually pronated. The idea was to turn the knuckles in the direction of the attack. This applies only to the true rapier and its descendants, not to edged cutting swords.

Since certain attacks can be stopped by only one particular parry, while others can be blocked by two or more, which one to choose is a matter of three things: (1) the type of the attack (cut or thrust, high or low, inside or outside); (2) how quickly we can respond; and (3) our intended action immediately following recovery (i.e., a counterattack or another parry). It goes without saying that the decision must be made in an instant. The nature of rapier combat is such that evading and counterthrusting are more often more useful than direct parrying and attacking.

This parry is believed to have developed from the action of unsheathing the weapon when attacked (in the urban setting of rapier combat, ambush, and surprise were not uncommon).

Although based on the heavier-handed cut-and-thrust movements, there are more variations to the rapier's major parries and angle attacks.

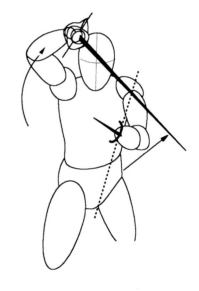

Parries may be small motions to redirect and ride off the incoming tip or they may be mechanically wider movements to scoop it up or knock it away (which may require withdrawing the tip).

More so than with a cutting sword, thrusting sword movements flow more fluidly from attack to parry to attack through beating, disengaging, and binding.

It is significant to note that, unlike with earlier swords, blocks with the rapier are made with the *edge* (because it is stronger on a thinner blade) and not the flat or back. Blocks are also made with the leading side (bottom or "true" edge) of the blade. Parrying with the "false side" (the top of the blade or thumb side) is less effective and not quite as strong. Many blocks can also be made by simply deflecting the hilt instead of with the length of the blade.

Basic dagger parry: dropping down or swiping to the left.

"Double parry" by crossing both weapons, possibly to trap the opponent's weapon.

Daggers can also be used to parry by trapping with their guards.

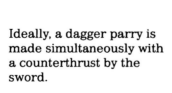

Ideally, a dagger parry is made simultaneously with a counterthrust by the sword.

High parry with counterthrust.

The method of defending with a rapier derives both from using a more agile weapon and defending more against attack by thrust. The new rapier techniques, having come from those used with wider, weightier cut-and-thrust swords, still retained some of their broad, heavy sweeping movements and parries. Because of this, in contrast to modern fencing, rapier action may be viewed as having somewhat less finesse. For safety reasons, practitioners today must tone down to a certain degree the force of their extensions and thrusts.

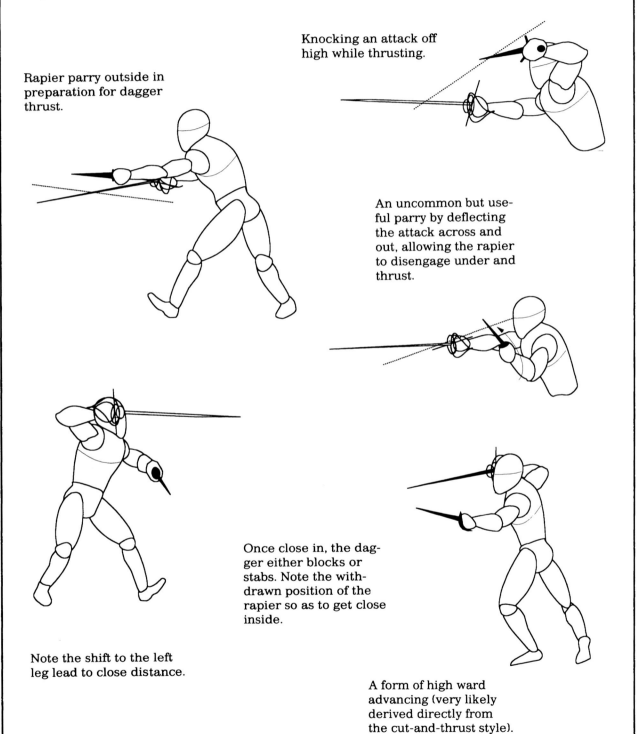

Knocking an attack off high while thrusting.

Rapier parry outside in preparation for dagger thrust.

An uncommon but useful parry by deflecting the attack across and out, allowing the rapier to disengage under and thrust.

Once close in, the dagger either blocks or stabs. Note the withdrawn position of the rapier so as to get close inside.

Note the shift to the left leg lead to close distance.

A form of high ward advancing (very likely derived directly from the cut-and-thrust style).

Parry with rapier by scooping or
deflecting the attack upward, and
then closing in with a dagger thrust.

Once a thrust has been deflected
enough, the hilt can also be used to
complete the block or bind the adversary's weapon.

Note that the left leg (rear leg) is
brought forward.

Because of its being less agile than
the modern sport variety, there is
often more call for a rapier to withdraw its tip off the attack and away
from the target when parrying (an
action avoided when possible). This
tends to occur more when facing
heavier, cutting swords. The farther
off the tip is moved, the slower any
counterattack will be.

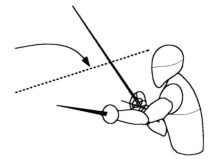

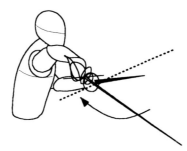

Facing multiple attackers or mass battle calls for a different approach and tactics than in single
combat. Although one weapon or sword such as the rapier may be well suited to duel, it may be
less useful in the hectic, chaotic confines of the battlefield. In single combat, a fighter can usually
take more time to ready himself and focus entirely upon the opponent at hand. Every factor of the
enemy and his weapon can be perceived and evaluated. In contrast, in the quicker pace of group
combat, this is not always possible. The enemy is usually armed with a wide array of weapon and
armor types, and combatants are scattered running in various directions. Attacks and threats can
come from all around. As soon as one opponent is dispatched, there is another, and all the while
fighting rages as the battle lines shift and maneuver. Such an environment is not ideal for a relatively "delicate" thrusting blade.

Handling a rapier involves a great deal of circular blade movement, consisting of thrusts, feints, and beats. Actions are also used that are similar to the bind in modern fencing. To close and disarm, a move is made to envelop and push a blade prior to thrusting.

An example of a basic circular parry or counterparry (sometimes known as a *contra cavatione* or *circolazione*).

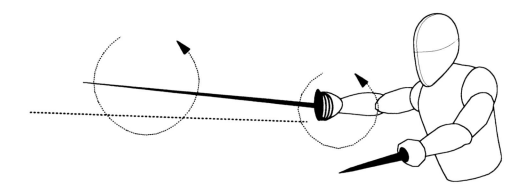

The circular parry developed out of a counterattack while the swordsman was maintaining his guard. It uses wider, deflecting motions of the blade and arm in knocking the adversary's blade down and away (out of line). It is used to block and prepare a counterattack. The motion can be clockwise to scoop up and out, or counterclockwise to deflect down and out. Unlike when used with a cutting blade, the point continues to be directed at the opponent. Though perhaps more common with the lighter small sword than with the rapier, the circular parry often can be used in tight situations.

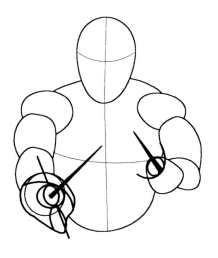

With the rapier, there are various means of pressuring the adversary's blade to force it *out of line* in preparation for a continued attack (such as in the "redoublement" of modern fencing). However, not all techniques used by rapier enthusiasts today are always "period" (historically accurate for the weapon). Some may be derived from small-sword moves or modern fencing, both of which have their own specific movements and tactics that may not be appropriate in historical (practical re-creational) rapier use. Rapier fighting cannot be described completely through reference to modern sport fencing's principles alone. Nor should stage combat's theatrics be viewed as legitimate source material.

It has been suggested that although it was the advent of firearms that ended the sword's supremacy as a weapon, ironically it also indirectly spurred advances in swordsmanship. As armor continued to decrease in value and popularity, it became necessary to better learn how to handle a sword in both offense and defense (i.e., the art of *fence*—from the Middle English *defence*).

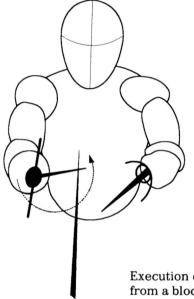

To attack, one must first *disengage* from a guard position. The disengage can be described as both a form of defense using the blade itself and a counteraction that preempts the adversary's move. It can be repeated (*double disengage*) or made with a larger motion over the top of a foe's weapon (a *coupe*). Either is commonly applied with quick feints and multiple attacks. The disengage is often met with a counterdisengage or semicircular parry. With thrusting swords, application of techniques often depends on the amount of contact or opposition (sometimes referred to as *stringering*) one has with the adversary's blade.

Execution of the highly used, basic disengage, moving the blade from a blocked to an open position (around and below the opponent's guard) in preparation for a thrust. It is said to have originally been developed from imitating the bobbing motions of fighting cocks. It redirects the attack's own thrusting force against it, pushing softly out and then reversing under and counterpushing.

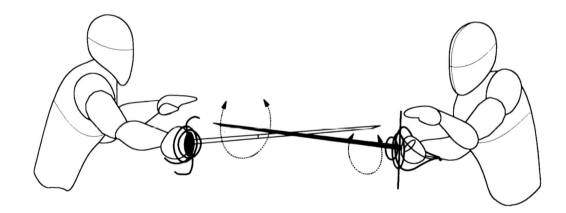

One of the fundamental actions is that of the beat (or *battere*). The beat is simply a quick smacking strike on the opposing blade to knock it aside or push the tip off line. It is a preparatory move to create an opening or invoke a response. It can even be made by the free hand or dagger. Variations of the beat are found in most forms of swordsmanship. It can be used in other forms to annoy, threaten or even disarm. The beat is also sometimes called *batement* or *passement*. Another move, which consisted of a sliding push followed by a beat or disengage on the adversary's blade, was known as an *intrecciata*.

RAPIER AND DAGGER

With a one-handed weapon that uses reach and quickness for thrusting attacks, a second hand weapon makes sense. Once the tip is deflected away or the opponent is entered in close, an alternative means of attack or defense is extremely useful. Also, some early rapiers were too heavy to effectively parry thrusts on their own. A second weapon greatly increases the ability to parry or trap and can further ward off an attacker. The combination of short and long blades effectively achieves this. Their use does require a good deal of coordination and adroitness (not to mention considerable footwork).

High ward advancing with dagger extended (as for an *imbroccata*).

With daggers, thrusts were the primary attack, cuts or slices having less value or opportunity for use.

Left leg leading and rapier withdrawn (as for a *stoccata*).

Dagger on high with rapier extended.

Naturally, most dagger use is close in. Daggers were used point up for greater defense, unlike in the medieval period where they were commonly held point down, often with the thumb over the pommel (possibly to add strength to a stab against armor).

Basic self-defense skill with the dagger was a necessity of the times. This is easily understood, considering the constraints of carrying a sword as well as the space and time requirements for drawing the long rapier.

Weapons at the ready, rapier leading.

Dagger leading at low guard/ward.

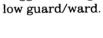

As common weapons and tools of utility, a wide range of parrying daggers or *main gauche* (left hand) were developed over time. Daggers, sometimes called *poniards*, were actually capable of being held in either hand. Average dagger lengths ranged from as short as 10 inches to as long as 24 inches; the daggers weighed between 1 and 2 pounds. Many had side rings or even sword guards. Having matching rapier and dagger sets (made *en suite*) was not uncommon.

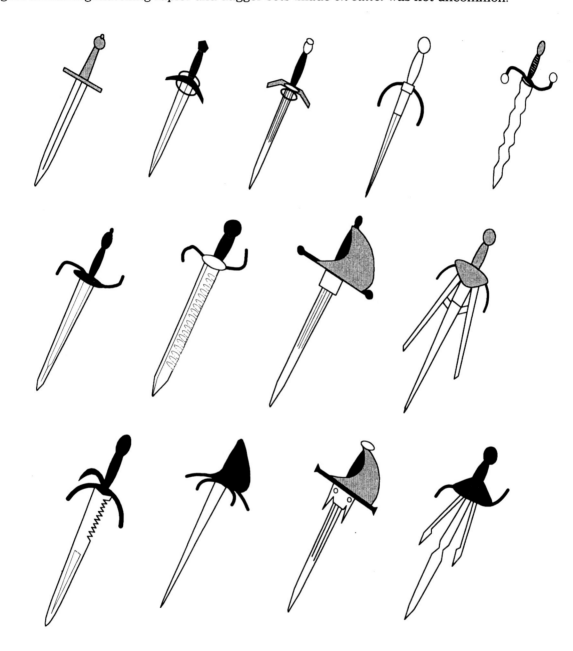

A variety were designed specifically for use with or against rapiers. Some versions of these had three-pronged blades or saw-like teeth to catch or possibly even break blades (the so-called sword breakers). However, these saw only limited use. There were also daggers with serrated edges to prevent them from being grabbed. Some forms of thrusting poniards had points only and no real edge. Of course, a dagger could always be thrown if the need arose. Today, a range of safe, flexible fencing daggers is available for practitioners to spar with.

The usual method of holding the close-hilted parrying dagger places the thumb behind the side ring with the guard sideways. This allows for effective movement and use in trapping. Daggers were also gripped in a normal full hand or with a finger around the ricasso.

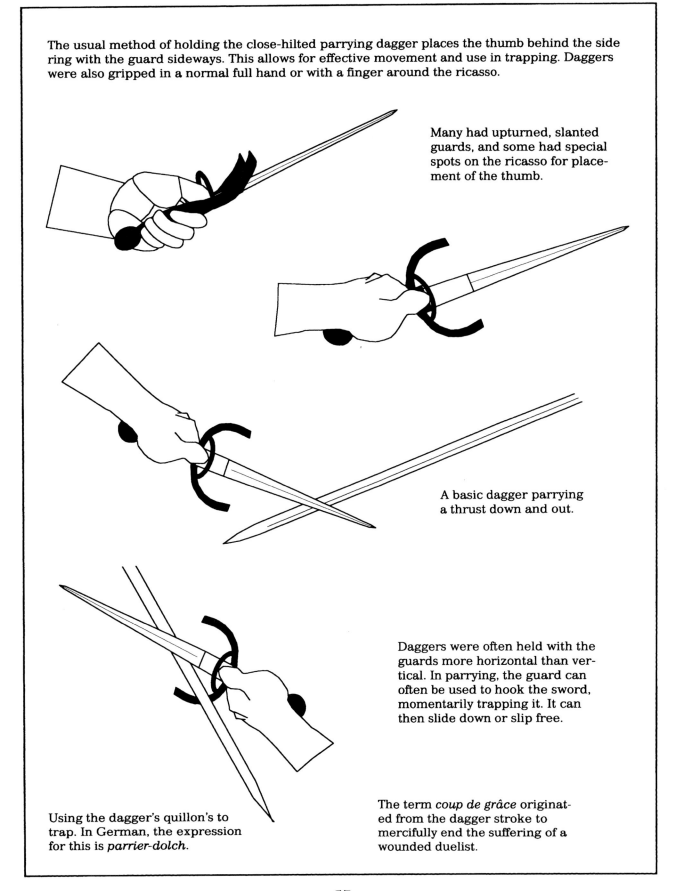

Many had upturned, slanted guards, and some had special spots on the ricasso for placement of the thumb.

A basic dagger parrying a thrust down and out.

Daggers were often held with the guards more horizontal than vertical. In parrying, the guard can often be used to hook the sword, momentarily trapping it. It can then slide down or slip free.

Using the dagger's quillon's to trap. In German, the expression for this is *parrier-dolch*.

The term *coup de grâce* originated from the dagger stroke to mercifully end the suffering of a wounded duelist.

FREE-HAND PARRYING

The rapier's lack of forceful cutting capacity allowed for a number of defensive slaps, deflects, and grabs by hand. Without a dagger, hand parrying (*battre de main*) was a viable substitute and was also faster. The use of a scabbard or a cane to parry with was also practiced.

Typical second
hand position.

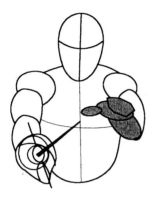

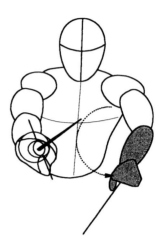

Block/deflect
down and out.

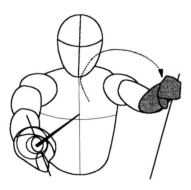

Deflect/grab
high and out.

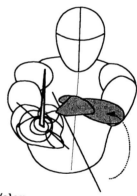

Block/slap
in and over.

The sword wielder often made hand parries while wearing a grasping glove or *guanto di presa* (a heavy leather or mail glove, or one with a mail-covered palm and fingers). Others were made of leather scales that overlapped backward so that thrusting tips could not easily get under them. Some were made of metal scales or had metal strips on the forearm. Occasionally, a full mail glove or metal gauntlet might be used. Being more useful on cutting blades, such gloves were less necessary against rapiers with little or no edge and so fell out of favor.

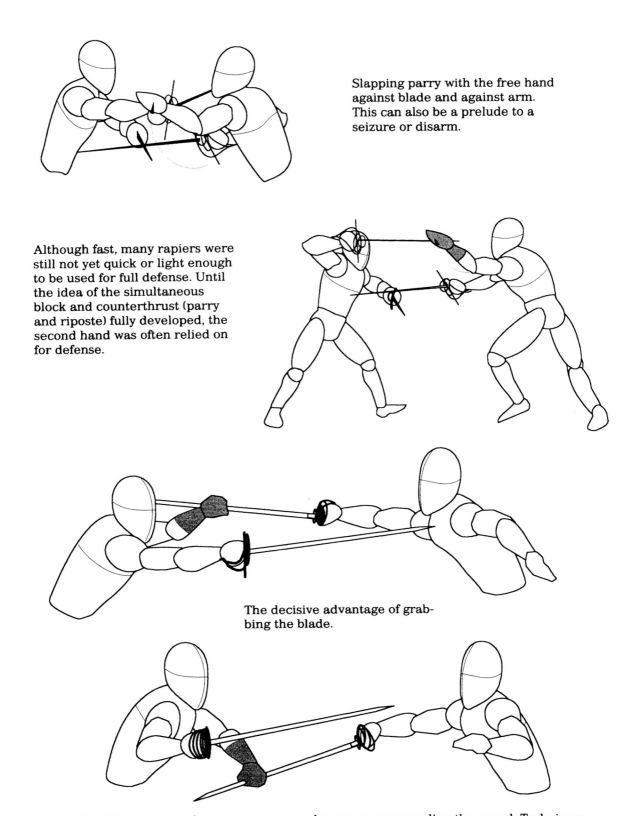

Slapping parry with the free hand against blade and against arm. This can also be a prelude to a seizure or disarm.

Although fast, many rapiers were still not yet quick or light enough to be used for full defense. Until the idea of the simultaneous block and counterthrust (parry and riposte) fully developed, the second hand was often relied on for defense.

The decisive advantage of grabbing the blade.

Getting hold of the opponent's weapon was once known as commanding the sword. Techniques and moves for grabbing (or seizure) were once called *grypes*.

RAPIER AND BUCKLER

Although used less frequently with the rapier, the small, hand-held shield provided a useful and challenging defense. Although it was better suited for defense against cuts, its surface area could make some thrusts difficult, and its parrying capacity allowed for deflecting or knocking blows. Some had various frontal points, hooks, or rings designed to entrap and even break rapier tips, and surely must have made fighting much more hazardous.

Bucklers were usually made of all metal (roughly 16 gauge), but some were made of wood with iron reinforcements.

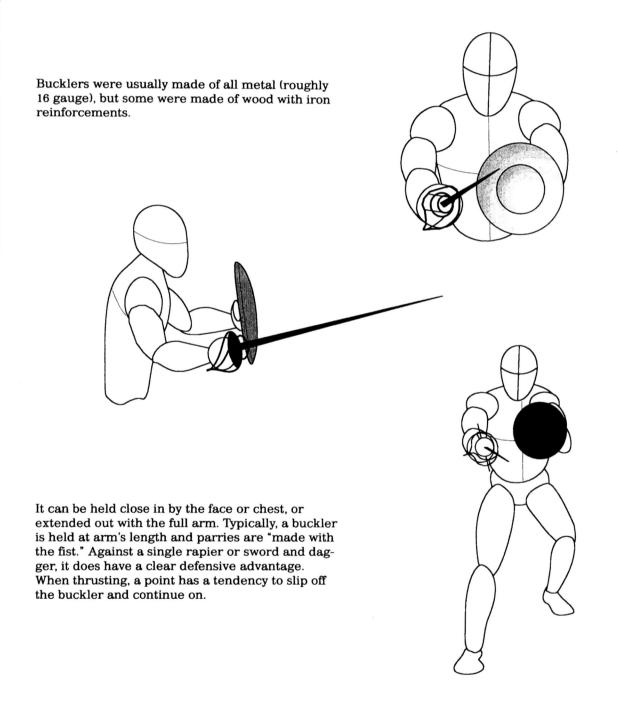

It can be held close in by the face or chest, or extended out with the full arm. Typically, a buckler is held at arm's length and parries are "made with the fist." Against a single rapier or sword and dagger, it does have a clear defensive advantage. When thrusting, a point has a tendency to slip off the buckler and continue on.

Bucklers were used more extensively with cut-and-thrust swords but were also not uncommon in the medieval period.

By the mid-1600s, bucklers, as well as gauntlets and even daggers, had fallen out of general use with the rapier.

Like strategy itself, which has its own contradictory logic, it is possible with a rapier to play off a buckler's very strength by attacking it. Many opponents, because they are so used to their adversaries naturally avoiding their bucklers at all cost, can be quite deficient in properly handling one. Thus, an attack may often be made directly against a buckler to provoke a move. This can be followed up with a disengage or change-in-line attack to the opening made. This principle can also be applied to a degree against daggers and even the enemy's own sword blade.

61

RAPIER AND CLOAK

A simple, common cloak or cape could be an effective implement in rapier fights. Its flexibility had defensive value. Cloaks were usually wrapped once or twice around the left arm. They could be tossed and waved to distract the attacker or entangle or "absorb" thrusts (this makes the most sense, considering the rapier's lack of cutting ability). Throwing it on the opponent's blade could weigh it down and thus help lower it out of line. It was even possible to envelop the opponent or obstruct his vision. The sword itself could be hidden or concealed to some degree, and the cloak could also "ride" on the tip and be thrown from it. Cloaks might even offer protection against minor cuts. It is also likely that rapiers must have punctured through them on occasion.

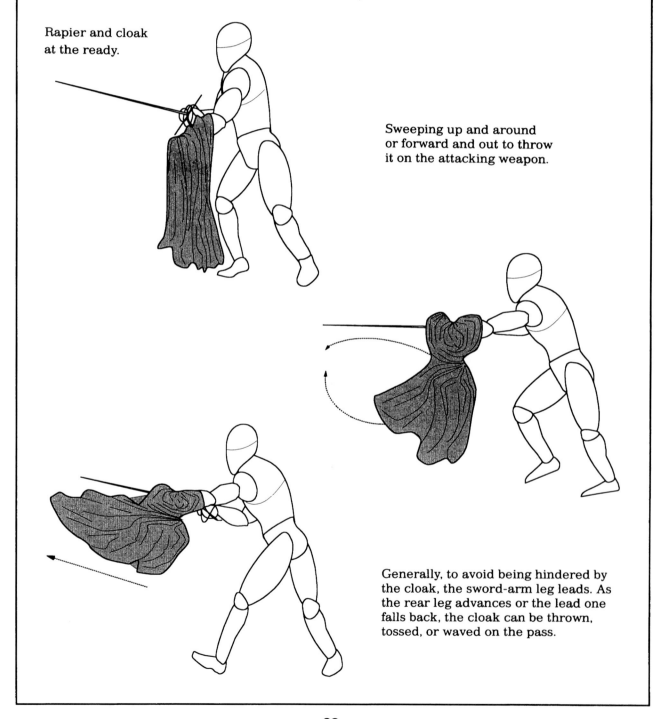

Rapier and cloak at the ready.

Sweeping up and around or forward and out to throw it on the attacking weapon.

Generally, to avoid being hindered by the cloak, the sword-arm leg leads. As the rear leg advances or the lead one falls back, the cloak can be thrown, tossed, or waved on the pass.

Deflecting thrusts
or parrying minor cuts.

Practitioners today can
use any large piece of strong
cloth to practice cloak techniques.

Wide, sweeping motions can trap, divert, or
slow the adversary's blade. A cloak could also
be used even while it was still being worn,
which may often have been the case in surprise attacks. It would, by necessity, have to
be pulled out of the way and held up by the
free hand.

USING TWO RAPIERS

The simultaneous use of two identical (left- and right-handed) rapiers was uncommon, but still known and respected. Because two swords were not normally worn, they were carried together in a case—hence, the term a *case of rapiers* or a *brace* (pair) *of rapiers*, also know as Florentine style (a Renaissance term popularly misapplied to medieval weaponry).

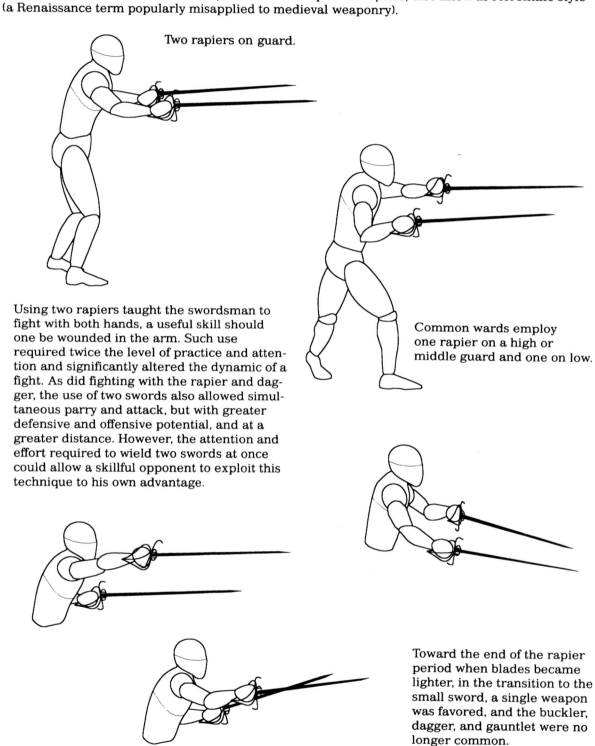

Two rapiers on guard.

Common wards employ one rapier on a high or middle guard and one on low.

Using two rapiers taught the swordsman to fight with both hands, a useful skill should one be wounded in the arm. Such use required twice the level of practice and attention and significantly altered the dynamic of a fight. As did fighting with the rapier and dagger, the use of two swords also allowed simultaneous parry and attack, but with greater defensive and offensive potential, and at a greater distance. However, the attention and effort required to wield two swords at once could allow a skillful opponent to exploit this technique to his own advantage.

Toward the end of the rapier period when blades became lighter, in the transition to the small sword, a single weapon was favored, and the buckler, dagger, and gauntlet were no longer common.

Distance (or measure) is often used as a form of buffer zone to judge, measure, and test the opponent. Making (or avoiding) an attack is a matter of discerning the proper distance and timing. The idea is to recognize and encourage gaps in the adversary's actions or reactions and use these to strike. Distance was sometimes described as being one in which a strike could be made either by a pass or lunge, by a simple step, or by just leaning in. Fundamentally, the rules of distance can be explained as stay out of reach to avoid being hit and never attack unless you are in range.
Just distance is the distance where if you are close enough to hit your opponent, he is also close enough to hit you. If you can perceive this and your opponent cannot (or at least if you can perceive it before he does), you have the advantage. Never come into this distance or let the opponent do so until you choose.

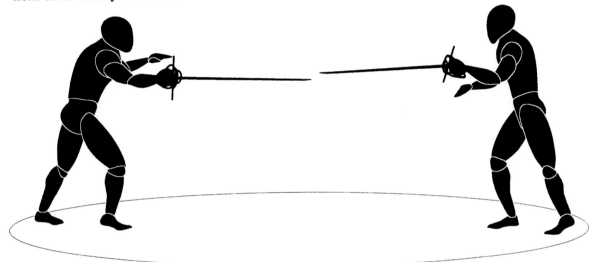

With a thrusting weapon, recovery—returning to a guarded (point-on) position—is particularly important. After making an attack or parry, recovery is necessary to continue on or change to another thrust or parry (as in the reprise of modern fencing). Recovery means to recover your readiness as well as your threat. Efficient action (economy of motion) is the objective. Action should naturally entail as little movement as necessary to quickly and accurately strike, block, or distract the adversary. With a rapier sword, which is heavier than a sport fencing blade, this can require an especially strong grip.

In any form of fighting, it is by causing the adversary to make mistakes that advantage is most often gained. This can be achieved by inducing the adversary to attack or commit while you lie in wait. One common method of doing this is to invite attack by feigning an opening or revealing a vulnerability (such as lowering the tip). The idea, obviously, is to cause a reaction that you are prepared to counter. The opponent must judge whether the opening is real or, if not, whether he can exploit it anyway. Many stances use a form of invitation. You must ensure that the feigned opening is not real and be ready to respond instantly if the bait is taken. There is always the danger of overexposing yourself. As has often been said, rather than relying on the adversary's inability to attack, you should rely instead on your ability to defend.

FIGHTING WITH THE RAPIER

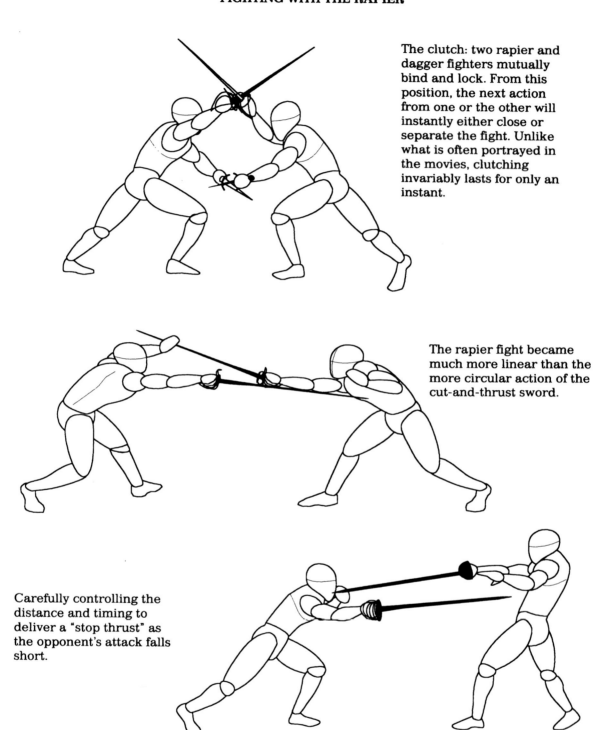

The clutch: two rapier and dagger fighters mutually bind and lock. From this position, the next action from one or the other will instantly either close or separate the fight. Unlike what is often portrayed in the movies, clutching invariably lasts for only an instant.

The rapier fight became much more linear than the more circular action of the cut-and-thrust sword.

Carefully controlling the distance and timing to deliver a "stop thrust" as the opponent's attack falls short.

Because it is a thrusting sword, reach is critical with the rapier. Once the opponent's point has been neutralized by being dodged or knocked away, a difference of only an inch or so can make a miss become a hit or a minor wound a kill. This reach is achieved not only by extending the arm, leaning, stepping, and, most important, lunging footwork, but also (as swordsmen learned) by the simple act of turning the torso. This pushes the shoulder out just that much farther. This can also be used in the reverse to avoid thrusts.

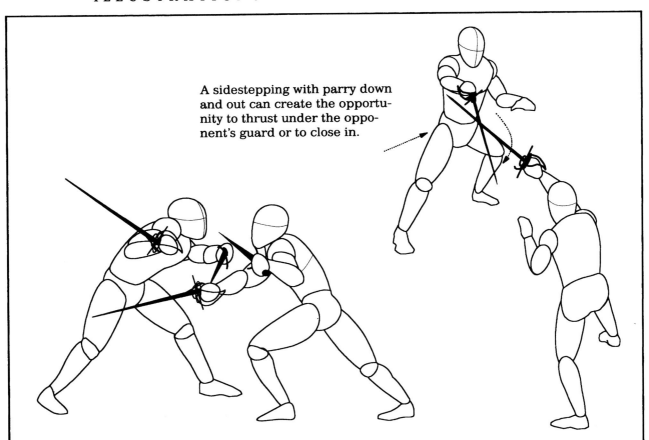

A sidestepping with parry down and out can create the opportunity to thrust under the opponent's guard or to close in.

When you have closed with an opponent and a clear thrust is impossible, merely slapping out with the blade is always an option. Though it would not seriously wound, the sting of the blow might be enough to distract the opponent, thereby creating the opening to withdraw and follow up with a better attack.

With open (or swept) hilts, the possibility exists for the adversary's point to pass through and become caught during thrusts. In this event, his blade can be trapped and broken. Though a broken rapier is still dangerous and may cause wounds, the act of snapping it free allows your own weapon to continue for a thrust. Some types of guard could also be used to trap an opponent's blade momentarily.

A dagger attack using a hip twist rear leg extension similar to boxing's cross punch.

The use of the *lunga* on offense.

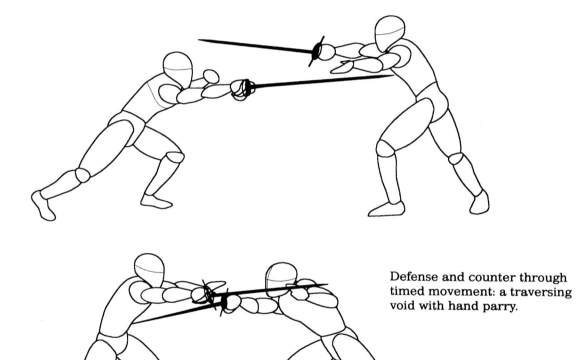

Defense and counter through timed movement: a traversing void with hand parry.

The various manuals by Renaissance Masters of Defence occasionally seem to overlook basic principles. Although currently available translations are imprecise, this is likely because of the assumption that basics would have been already known to the reader. Despite their universal commonalties, the variety in style among the masters allows practitioners reconstructing Renaissance swordsmanship today to explore numerous approaches without necessarily being incorrect or wrong. Differences among modern enthusiasts can be due more to the practice system and sparring rules being employed rather than any methodology.

CUT-AND-THRUST SWORDS

Examples of typical cut-and-thrust swords showing the early development of the compound guard, including finger ring, knuckle bow, recurved guards, and arms of the hilt. These likely grew out of the need to control the point, protect the unarmored hand, and defend more against thrusts. Note the wide but beginning-to-taper blades. Handles also tended to be shorter than with medieval swords.

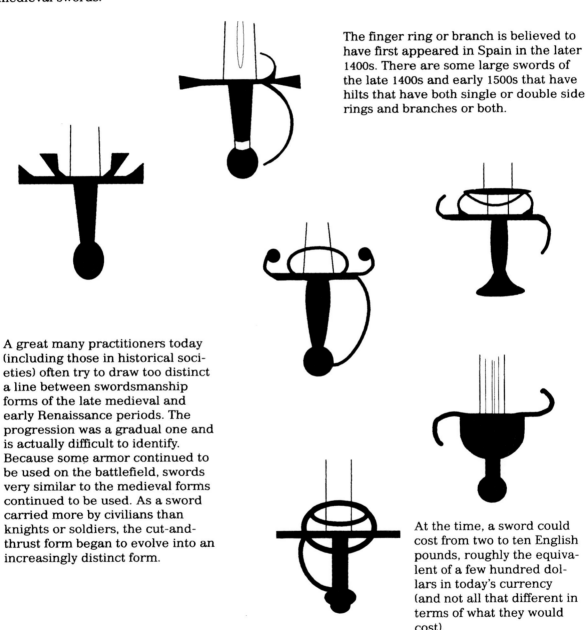

The finger ring or branch is believed to have first appeared in Spain in the later 1400s. There are some large swords of the late 1400s and early 1500s that have hilts that have both single or double side rings and branches or both.

A great many practitioners today (including those in historical societies) often try to draw too distinct a line between swordsmanship forms of the late medieval and early Renaissance periods. The progression was a gradual one and is actually difficult to identify. Because some armor continued to be used on the battlefield, swords very similar to the medieval forms continued to be used. As a sword carried more by civilians than knights or soldiers, the cut-and-thrust form began to evolve into an increasingly distinct form.

At the time, a sword could cost from two to ten English pounds, roughly the equivalent of a few hundred dollars in today's currency (and not all that different in terms of what they would cost).

Although many Renaissance military swords (and medieval ones as well) are occasionally referred to generically as *broadswords*, this is inaccurate. Though useful, this common term was actually first used by collectors in the Victorian era to distinguish wider blades from thinner ones. There is also a form of short 18th- and 19th-century cutlass known as the true broadsword. The various terms for cutlass are much older themselves and were applied to a range of weapons.

Lighter, thinner military swords were becoming more suitable for civilian wear and use. As with medieval swords, those that can be qualified as early Renaissance cut-and-thrust (transition) swords exist in great variety. Their characteristics generally consist of narrower, lighter, double-edged blades tapering to sharp points with weights of 1.5 to 2.5 pounds and overall lengths of approximately 37 to 45 inches. As with any sword, length and feel are more a matter of the personal preference of the wielder. Whether or not a sword can be classified as cut-and-thrust or rapier depends upon its blade width, edge shape, and balance—not its hilt design.

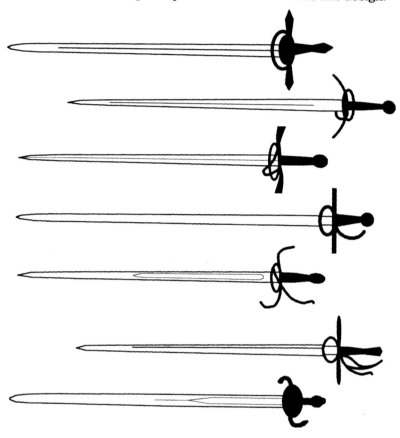

Cross-sections of two kinds of cut-and-thrust blade shapes compared with a common medieval sword form. Note the rib-like raised fullers (risers) and different widths.

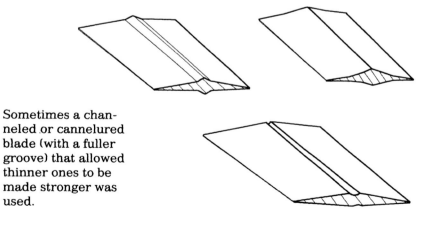

Sometimes a channeled or cannelured blade (with a fuller groove) that allowed thinner ones to be made stronger was used.

A cut-and-thrust sword must be just wide and heavy enough to make cutting blows, yet light and slender enough for agile thrusts. Typically, these swords were double edged. A number of wide, saber-like curved blades also saw use at the time, although they were little more than meat cleavers.

The typical cut-and-thrust grip is somewhat looser than that of earlier medieval swords so as to allow for more maneuverability. One goes from stab to slice and back again. Looping the finger over the ricasso was common for control. The ricasso is typically blunted and squared off. The "fingering grip" method used on most cut-and-thrust swords enables it to be more manageable and agile than earlier medieval weapons. The significance of this simple change in gripping should not be underappreciated.

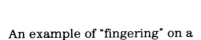

An example of "fingering" on a medieval sword.

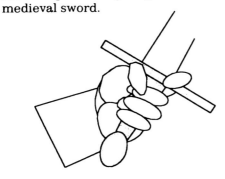

An obvious danger exists of getting a finger hacked off or the opponent's blade sliding down on it.

The grip for modern saber fencing places the thumb on the back of the handle. Note the shape and thinness of the blade. The saber's bell guard (or *caprice*) evolved from the knuckle bar.

An example of a hand position for gripping a cut-and-thrust style sword. Note the contrast for a thrust using the "fist" grip on a slashing medieval sword. This common means of gripping can also be used with a cut-and-thrust sword.

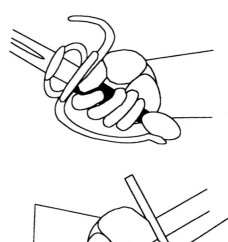

A good replica cut-and-thrust Renaissance sword is not as easy to find as are other types. Practitioners are warned to avoid the many costume swords on the market. The majority of these reproductions are inaccurate, poorly tempered blades of inferior steel. Most also lack proper weight and balance. The peddlers of these often insanely priced trash swords (for that is what most are) are not about to inform their potential customers of these facts. Buy only quality replicas.

Additionally, excluding staged fights, no serious method of safe contact sparring has really yet emerged for cut-and-thrust swordsmanship the way it has for rapier fencing or medieval fighting. Practitioners today must either rely on the limitations of staged combat and fencing weapons or else develop new alternatives.

USE OF THE RENAISSANCE CUT-AND-THRUST SWORD

Taking advantage of a sword's thrusting capability tends to promote stances that favor greater reach. This can be achieved by leading with the sword-arm leg forward (in a more sideways position than that used with a larger shield). Using a buckler or a dagger also suggests a form that requires more mobility than with the older shield-and-sword method. Most cut-and-thrust sword strikes were made "on the pass," using a simultaneous forward or sidestepping move with the rear leg passing over the lead. This can add reach and power to a cut, but also tends to announce its arrival.

Evasive movements are necessary because of the relative slowness (in contrast to later small swords and modern fencing weapons) of cut-and-thrust swords (and some rapiers) when parrying in line.

Stepping into a strike is preferably done to the adversary's outside, away from his second weapon and to his exposed leg, sword arm, flank, or rear.

If no second weapon is used, occasionally the free hand is held out of the way and even holds the scabbard or rests on the hip (as in some later sword forms).

The manuals of the cut-and-thrust sword masters reveal the precursors of techniques that were to become the rapier's specialty. Naturally, many of the concepts found in these early manuals are more easily and clearly understood after practice-cutting with a blade of the true cut-and-thrust variety. Although the manuals on the Renaissance sword are not as in-depth as later ones on the rapier, the method is not difficult to re-create. Handling the weapons, sparring, and practice cutting all reveal the essential mechanics.

Note the wider sweeping motions applied in delivering cutting slashes and making smacking parries with the broader cut-and-thrust type of sword. The weapon is held predominantly at a 45-degree angle to allow both defense against thrusts and ease of parrying cuts. While remaining in a point-on threat (thrust) position to the opponent, the swordsman can still parry and counter with little motion required. The 45-degree middle-guard position also allows for the application of draw-cuts or for the arm to be raised for basic cutting strikes. Keep in mind, however, that proper movement is impossible to illustrate through still pictures alone.

The general concept is to freely and strongly strike the opponent without having to first block with the weapon and then return an attack. Rather, the weapon is withheld and cuts are timed so as to fake the opponent into misparrying, overreaching, or otherwise opening himself up. As with most any sword (or hand-held striking weapon), a great number of feints and cutovers (sometimes also called changes in line of attack) are employed to mislead the adversary.

Generally, one watches the opponent's torso because there is nowhere it goes that the rest of the body does not follow. The ideal, though, is to take everything into view peripherally and not focus on any one thing. Some say to watch an opponent's wrist or grip or even the face or eyes. However, skillful fighters will reveal nothing through their gaze, and against multiple opponents you cannot take time to look at all of them.

Advances, retreats, and side steps involve turning or pivoting on the foot.

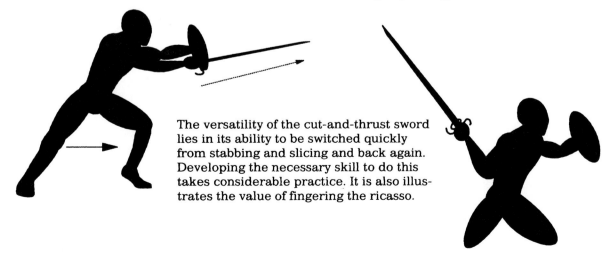

The versatility of the cut-and-thrust sword lies in its ability to be switched quickly from stabbing and slicing and back again. Developing the necessary skill to do this takes considerable practice. It is also illustrates the value of fingering the ricasso.

THE FUNDAMENTAL STANCES

The basic postures, wards, and ready positions (high, low, middle, outside) all flow one to another and can lead with either leg. Though it may vary with personal style, any stance is merely a form of these few. More than being guards, stances are attitudes for both offense and defense.

The proper stance is that which is most effective and comfortable for the user with the shoulder relaxed, knees slightly bent, and the elbow not too far out or too close in to the body.

High.

Middle (sometimes held more horizontally).

From the middle guard, the sword is pointed at the adversary's midsection or chest.

Low (sometimes known as *terza* and held more horizontally).

High outside (also known as *reverse, guardant,* or *prima*).

Outside (or "open guard").

Although a classic medieval sword could conceivably be used with the same basic stances, cuts, and parries, in doing so it would not be used nearly as agilely or fluidly as a leaner, true cut-and-thrust blade.

A low-outside ward that, although it appears open, allows for a number of strong and effective countercuts. Diagonal strikes may be delivered upward left to right or with a turn of the wrist brought over diagonally and down left to right. The blade may also be lifted to parry with the pommel up before counterattacking. All of these can be employed on the pass, as either the rear leg steps forward or the lead leg falls back.

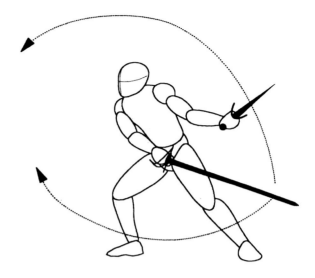

In the Elizabethan period, schools of arms taught by "Masters of Defence" thrived. Spanish and Italian masters were well respected and sought after. Schools and guilds in Germany were already well established and in circa 1570 included the Federfechter, an association of rapier fighters and rivals of the famous Marxbruder. Early fencing schools had generally unsavory reputations as hangouts for ruffians and rogues. Henry the VIII made an English school of fencing (for sword and buckler) official in 1540. The Corporation of Masters of the Science of Defence (or the Masters of Defense guild), dedicated to instruction with numerous swords and weapons, had its own regulations and codes. It had four levels of fighters: Scholar, Free Scholar, Provost, and Master. The "blue collar" English master at arms had to earn his title through rigorous public trial of his skill called "playing the prize." This could consist of dozens of bouts with a variety of swords and weapons against numerous opponents.

In England during the 1700s and 1800s, professional men-at-arms and swordsmen known as "prizefighters" would stage public duels for cash awards. Though using blunted weapons, most of these were quite bloody affairs, and many ended in death. Unarmed bouts were added, and as they gained in popularity, weapon use fell off. Eventually, these contests grew into the modern sport of boxing. These gladiator-like shows, often put on by mere street ruffians and brawlers, are not to be confused with the earlier, more noble prize fights that Masters of Defence and their students participated in for advancement during the 1500s and early 1600s.

CUTTING AND STRIKING

The basic 45-degree on-guard position or posture. From here the sword can make any parry to any area, deliver draw cuts, or simply lift at the elbow or shoulder to strike. These are all applied in conjunction with properly stepping into or out of the opponent's action.

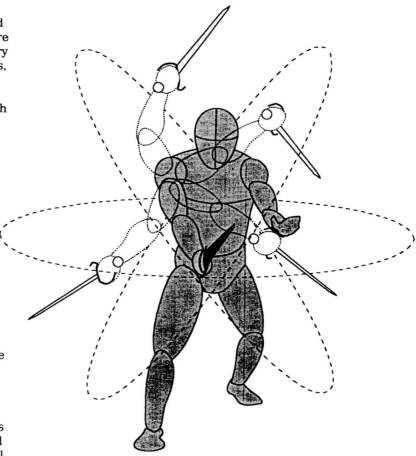

In combat on the Renaissance field of battle, the same basic cut-and-thrust principles could essentially still have been used on armored opponents—except that the strikes should have been harder, and draw-cuts were far less useful. The parries and cuts shown here, while similar in movement, are not those of later broadswords and curved sabers.

Circles representing the major paths a sword in *one* hand follows as it cuts and returns to parry or cut again.

Sword strikes are about cutting, trying to cleave and shear into flesh and bone. It is not simply throwing the blade out there or hammering with it. Generally, cuts can be delivered from the shoulder (sometimes called *arrebatar* in the Spanish schools), which, though slower, have more power. Those made from the elbow (mediatajo) are quicker but have less power and are perhaps better suited for draw-cuts and close-in moves. Cutting from the "wrist" is quickest but also weakest. Striking with the full arm in a wider arc from higher positions may be best applied in conjunction with evading and countering. From the middle positions at closer distances, cutting from the lower arm may often be applied immediately after parrying, deflecting, or evading. If a cut connects, the swordsman must follow through; if it misses, he must recover (or prepare for a parry). Unarmored human limbs need not be dismembered or hacked to the bone to be rendered useless in a fight. They can often be effectively immobilized with slicing flesh wounds. The wrists, inner elbows, underarms, triceps, calves, and the sides or backs of the knees are particularly vulnerable. If ligaments or tendons are cut, such wounds could be permanent.

The various cuts and thrusts, known by many terms, were given names by the Italian masters. They were sometimes called *mandritta* (right to left cut) or *reversa* (left to right), and could be delivered diagonally (*squalembrato*), vertically (*fendente*), horizontally (*tonda*), and straight up (*montante*). Additionally, there were the basic thrusts (*punta*) to the adversary's left and right guards.

Cuts left to right:
Reversa

Cuts from right to left
Mandritti

Fendente
(downward vertical)

Squalembrato
(diagonal downward)

Squalembrato
(diagonal downward)

Tonda
(horizontal)

Tonda
(horizontal)

Squalembrato
(diagonal upward with true edge)

Squalembrato
(diagonal upward with true edge)

Montante
(vertical upward)

There were cuts known as *falso manco* for cuts to the knees or wrists with the false edge, *falso dritto* for cuts to the wrists with the false edge, and *montante sotto mano* for an upward cut with the false edge.

Almost all cuts were made as *dritto filo*, or with the true (right) edge. False-edge attacks (*falso filo*) or diagonal upward cuts using the back of the sword (the false edge) were not uncommon. Though they are weaker cuts, they can be quick, and the target areas can be exposed. False-edge attacks are, for the most part, mechanically weaker. A simple turn of the wrist on upward diagonal cuts can turn them into stronger true-edge attacks. The Italian master Carronza had one cut known as the *manoble*, a light slash of the point delivered by a flick of the wrist. It could be made against the hand, forearm, or face. With the rapier, such blows (like the *stromazone*) were mere slashing cuts and not lethal.

77

Cuts are best done with the first third of the blade (closest to the tip). This is the "point-of-percussion" for a straight, long, single-handed cutting blade. Both edges are used, but the top edge much less so. Force is added to cuts by putting the hips and body weight behind the blow. Though delivered at about 45-degree angles for best cutting effect, they can strike at any viable area in between. Primary cuts are delivered to the head, collar, shoulders, and waist. Preferred targets also include the calf and back of the knee, inner thigh, elbow, wrist, and neck. Against any armored opponents that cut-and-thrust swords might encounter, cuts would presumably be aimed at the unarmored sections and the joints or even possibly deferred in favor of certain thrusts.

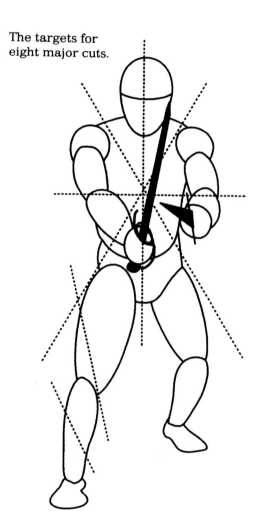

The targets for eight major cuts.

What is important in practicing real cut-and-thrust swordsmanship is that which is most often ignored today: the cutting. It is surprising how many enthusiasts who, while owning swords, have never even attempted to do any cutting. Practicing actual cutting with a sword must not be neglected. Not test-cutting is like practicing driving without ever starting the car. Of course, it is often impractical to accomplish, because not every practitioner can obtain a decent sword, get a sharp edge on it, and then locate substantial materials to cut. This is unfortunate, because cutting, like sparring, reveals a multitude of weaknesses, bad habits, and incorrect techniques. It is the key to discovering many obscure and subtle aspects of swordsmanship (e.g., breathing, focus, flow, follow-through). In fact, in a sense, it shows what swordsmanship is all about; many moves make sense only when seriously cutting with a live blade.

It is most strongly suggested that serious practitioners obtain and try using a quality replica blade (not just stage-combat versions made for beating on each other). Among materials good for practice cutting are 1/4-to-1/2-inch-thick cardboard tubes, densely rolled newspaper, rolled-up straw mats, fresh bamboo, and even compressed wet foam or soft plant stalks of sufficient diameter.

The original significance of pronation and supination lies in the use of the edge of the cut-and-thrust sword form. It makes the most sense when viewed in this way only. Guards were often known by the position of the blade's edge. The issue of supination or pronation therefore, is subordinate to the simple intuitive understanding that to cut, you must aim the sword's *edge* at the target. To best parry you move to use the flat.

Either diagonal cut can also be a horizontal one.

Diagonal left to right.

Diagonal right to left.

Reverse, cutting up right to left.

Upward diagonal cuts are harder to employ by the nature of their angle. They are also somewhat harder to parry for this same reason. If misjudged, it is easy to accidentally move the grip into the path of the attack.

During practice in the schools (particularly with the rapier), the concept of "scholar's privilege" was often observed, wherein inexperienced students were not struck in the face. During prize fights, blows below the waist were generally forbidden. This observance was often followed even in street brawls. Naturally, for duels to the death, battlefield combat, or other lethal encounters, these "rules" were discarded. It can be assumed that instruction took this into account. Considering that armor breastplates were still in use, practicing attacks to the arms and legs would be obvious.

These cuts, invariably using a forward or side step, have essentially the same motion whether delivered from the shoulder (with the full arm) or from the elbow (primarily by the forearm and wrist). Delivering cuts from the elbow is possible with a lighter blade that is balanced more at the hilt, but they are not decisive and must have rarely killed anyone in a single blow.

This preliminary position may turn into a diagonal cut, a vertical cut, or even a thrust.

An example of a horizontal cut (right to left) or *tonda*.

When it comes to training in the relatively uncommon form of cut-and-thrust swordsmanship, contact sparring is essential. No one would think of learning fencing without ever making touches on his opponent, and the same can be said for cut-and-thrust swordsmanship. Enthusiasts today have a range of options for pursuing this (varying in degree of historical accuracy and physical intensity). While actual live-steel training is highly recommended for test-cutting, these swords can't be used for practical sparring purposes. Blunts or dulled versions (stage-combat swords) offer valuable aspects but, again, are inherently limited for cut-and-thrust sparring because of the danger involved (although practicing with them certainly teaches finesse and control). The same can also be said for wooden weapons as substitutes. Bamboo versions are ridiculously light and behave far too unrealistically, as do silly foam swords. Padded contact weapons (when properly weighted and balanced) offer an excellent alternative if constructed with a discernible "edge." However, they do not simulate the feel and blade play of true swords well enough to offer a complete picture. In the end, a swordsman should endeavor to supplement his preferred method by cross-training with others. Training exclusively with only one means of sparring is limiting and eventually leads to a narrower interpretation of both technique and fighting.

FEINTS

The heavier the blade, the more difficult feinting (or "falsing" as it was known) is. Although a feint (*finda* in Italian) is fairly obvious, it can be defined as a false move or faked blow that changes its line of attack to another target that it opens up. A swordsman feints high, strikes low, fakes left, cuts right, raises but thrusts, etc. Often he even throws multiple feints. The idea is to outmaneuver the opponent by overwhelming his sense of timing and thus to prevent a proper defense or counter. The opponent naturally mistakes the false move and either reacts to it, and thereby uncovers himself, or discovers it too late to respond accordingly. Against novice fighters, a feint can also be used to test how they handle themselves. The problem with feints, however, is that a skilled adversary will recognize them and not react, or that an unskilled adversary will not know that he should react. In either case, the attempt can leave the one doing the feinting vulnerable to counterattack.

Ideally, feints should contain just enough commitment so as to appear real, but not so much that they prevent a real follow-up. Changing the path of a strike as it is committed is also a form of feinting. The more skillful the fighter, the more easily he can alter a blow's direction and make a change-in-line of attack. Feints are not an end in themselves but, rather, a means of preparation. The more skillful a fighter, the less he will rely on feints, choosing instead to counterstrike. Sometimes feints are used only to test and probe the opponent's reactions, to calibrate his sensitivity to both real and false attacks. When skilled fighters engage, feints often become much shorter and can even consist of mere flinches (which can instantly turn into an actual strike or vice versa). To a master fighter, it often does not matter whether an attack is a feint or genuine; he can counter it all the same.

EXAMPLES OF PRIMARY CUT-AND-THRUST PARRIES

It is vital to realize that parries with a sword are made with the *flat of the blade* and *not* the edge, as is commonly mistaken (this is typical of modern saber fencing and common in stage combat). Edges need to be kept sharp and free of nicks or gouges. They are too weak to be intentionally placed in the path of oncoming strikes. Doing so will likely break them far sooner. Parrying with the stronger flat side requires only a slight turn of the wrist. In fact, this is the very reason swords are made to flex.

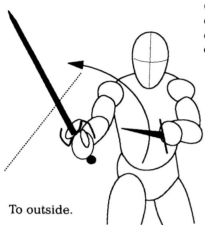

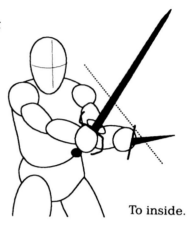

The general rule of parrying can be expressed as follows: *deflect rather than block and evade rather than deflect.*

To outside.

To inside.

Parries to the left and right can be employed equally well against vertical or horizontal cuts.

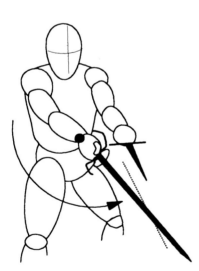

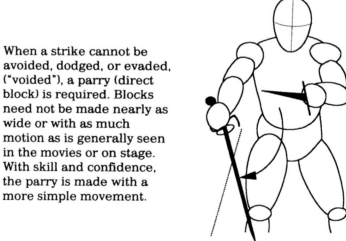

When a strike cannot be avoided, dodged, or evaded, ("voided"), a parry (direct block) is required. Blocks need not be made nearly as wide or with as much motion as is generally seen in the movies or on stage. With skill and confidence, the parry is made with a more simple movement.

To low inside.

To low outside.

Parries were rarely defined in exact terms. They were described more as basic defensive reactions than as sword placement. Although cut-and-thrust parries are reminiscent of those used in modern saber fencing and its precedents, they are not equivalent.

For most parries, rather than move the whole weapon over or out to meet the attack, only the blade and tip need move while the hilt remains more or less in the same position. For others, the opposite may be true.

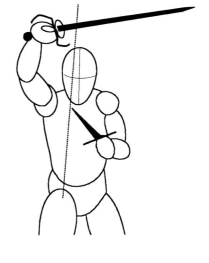

Variation
to high.

To high inside
from below.

Both of these "sliding parries" can allow the blow to glance off, preparing the way for a countercut. They are also made with the flat of the blade, not the edge.

In any parrying, the arm should not be rigid or fully extended, or the block will be weak. The grip should also not be too loose or too tight. There must be suppleness in the arm in order for it to resist.

To middle thrust (this can also be used against vertical cuts).

Parrying is nearly always done in conjunction with footwork. Generally, one can step to the side against vertical cuts, step back to let lateral cuts pass, or step in to stifle or preempt either.

Far more so than with either medieval swords or rapiers, the use of draw-cuts (slicing pulls) is more common with a cut-and-thrust blade. This is because of its lighter heft and its point being aimed at the opponent more often. With such techniques, beats and parries can be easily turned offensive by strongly pressing the blade forward and sliding it across. Quicker than strikes and still able to keep the point in-line, they are useful, effective actions against unarmored targets. draw-cut target areas are those of opportunity, but include chiefly the abdomen, forearms and elbows, underarms, neck and face, calves, and knees.

Slipping past and slicing across the abdomen as the adversary steps in. This can be applied on either side.

Push cuts (sliding forward slices) are also possible, but inherently have less force. It is also advisable to move out and away with a draw-cut, thereby avoiding the adversary's own weapon, rather than to move in for a push.

Because raising the arm and weapon to cut can leave one vulnerable, a quicker blade can make much greater use of slices and draw-cuts (on unarmored targets) rather than hacks and slashes. Because cut-and-thrust swords are one-handed weapons, techniques for their use can differ noticeably from those gripped with two hands. Many cut-and-thrust sword hilts also restrict the grip somewhat and thereby tend to facilitate slices more than hacks.

Stepping in to block or preempt
and then delivering a draw cut. It is
also possible to counter by directly
attacking the opponent's own blade
as he cuts.

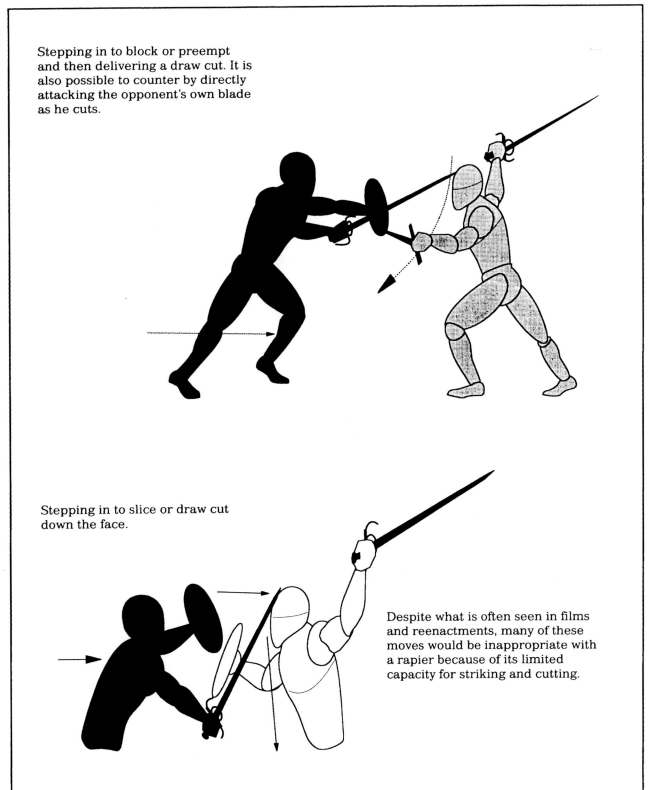

Stepping in to slice or draw cut
down the face.

Despite what is often seen in films
and reenactments, many of these
moves would be inappropriate with
a rapier because of its limited
capacity for striking and cutting.

Even a small cut to the unprotected head can be enough of a blow to leave the adversary momentarily vulnerable. At the very least, the cut could be distracting because bleeding from the head
often irritates the eyes and disrupts vision.

Some useful but more difficult techniques of cut-and-thrust swords are those that involve countercutting by deflecting rather than parrying. This form of counterattack was not uncommon. As the adversary strikes, a blow is made to knock his blade aside as it comes in. The ideal is to smack the attack away (to the outside or inside) and then make an immediate return cut all in one basic motion. This requires not only precise control of timing and sense of distance, but also quick steps to move out of and then back into the attack. Deflecting an attack and countercutting in this way take great skill as well as a light, sturdy weapon.

Note: Because the simultaneous nature of the movements involved, it is difficult to express countercutting examples in either words or illustrations.

The technique can be applied against attacks to the right or to the left.

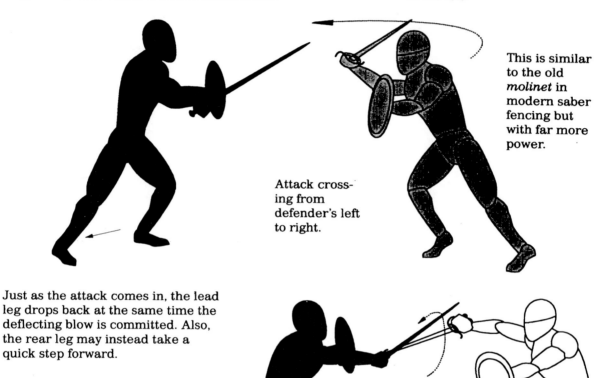

This is similar to the old *molinet* in modern saber fencing but with far more power.

Attack crossing from defender's left to right.

Just as the attack comes in, the lead leg drops back at the same time the deflecting blow is committed. Also, the rear leg may instead take a quick step forward.

The deflecting parry comes from behind the attack and in the same direction (i.e., crossing right to left, left to right). It is aimed essentially on the first third of the attacker's blade and functions like a half-circular parry.

As the opponent's sword is knocked aside, the opening is made to cut or strike back. If no opening is made, the technique serves simply as another form of defense. This manner of deflecting and countering is applied continuously or in combination with direct blocking and circular parries (made with a cut-and-thrust sword by essentially swirling around the point).

Coordinating your timing and distance with the adversary's attack is a fundamental principle. Known as "voiding," it is more than just a means of defensive evading and readying a counter-stroke. It is a matter of stepping out of or into the opponent's range to deliver a countercut or thrust. It is a means of controlling distance through traverse steps so as to attack openings in the opponent's action.

Just as you have judged that the adversary is committed to an attack, your lead leg falls back as you bring a countercut forward. Judgment of distance and true intention are vital here. This is also important afterward to follow up or recover. By dropping back with the lead leg in this manner, power can be generated in the hips and shoulders for a counter-cut. This can also mask your true reach and mobility. The body's weight may also be brought down on the blow.

A variation is to drop back with a "hop" of both legs and bring the sword down or around simultaneously. Again, should the blow miss or be parried, quick and smooth recovery is necessary for an additional void or cut.

Stepping out can also be made diagonally so as to widen the distance from the attack and give more room to maneuver. Stepping quickly back into the opponent with a pass can ensure an effective counterattack. In this way, voiding and passing are really mutual actions.

The flow of this kind of sword fight can be one of continuous voids, passes, and wide, quick steps as each fighter throws mutual cuts, thrusts, and smacking or punching parries.

BUCKLERS

The good defense against cuts and thrusts provided by the small hand shield buckler made it useful and popular. The weapon could also be used to deliver blows. Essentially, daggers use the same fundamental buckler parries.

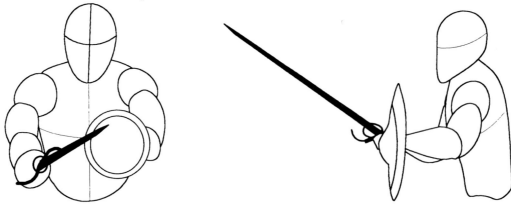

The English word *buckler* is derived from an Old French word (*bocle*) for the metal boss (or *umbo*) on a shield. Italian bucklers were known as *bochiero* or *rotella*. Highly maneuverable with a single handle in the middle (*enarme*), a buckler could be carried far more easily than larger shields by civilians. A raised boss over the handle was usual. Bowl-like concave versions were also known to exist. At night, lanterns could even be hung on bucklers and were also used to blind and distract opponents.

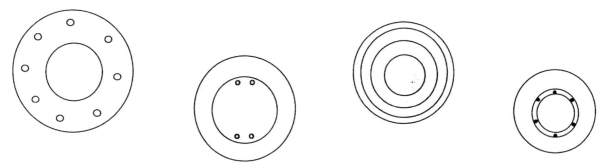

Bucklers came in various shapes (round was most common) and ranged from roughly 8 to 18 inches. The most common seem to have been 10 to 12 inches in diameter and under four pounds. Practice bucklers can be easily made today out of either wooden boards, metal pot lids, or even hubcaps. They can be padded for safety or left natural. Authentic replicas are also available.

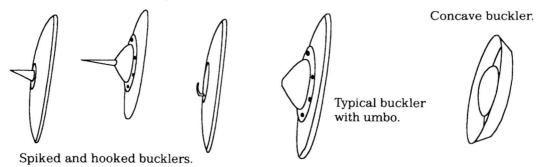

Concave buckler.

Typical buckler with umbo.

Spiked and hooked bucklers.

Sword-and-buckler fighting was a popular pastime for ruffians and restless youths. Some sword and buckler fights were simply armed brawls that ended without significant wounds. The term *swashbuckler* comes from the sound made by a buckler worn on the belt as it swishes against the scabbard as the wearer walks. Pointed bucklers were outlawed in England in 1562 as part of an effort to discourage dueling and injury.

SWORD AND BUCKLER

With a small hand-held shield, a strong grip is needed to parry the hard blows of a sword. Because of the shield's size, it's possible to lead with either leg forward.

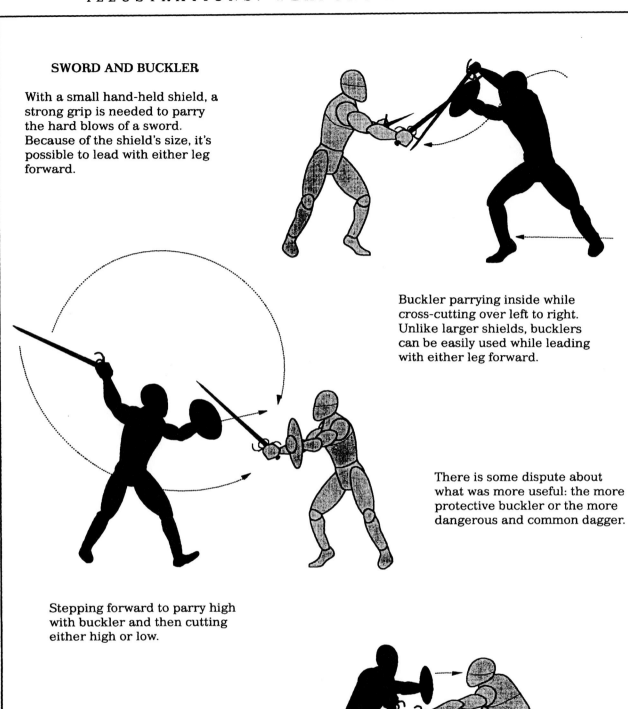

Buckler parrying inside while cross-cutting over left to right. Unlike larger shields, bucklers can be easily used while leading with either leg forward.

There is some dispute about what was more useful: the more protective buckler or the more dangerous and common dagger.

Stepping forward to parry high with buckler and then cutting either high or low.

Stepping in and dropping the blade to parry down and out. This allows for a counterstrike or buckler hit as you pass behind the opponent.

At its core, swordsmanship is not about complexity; it is about simplifying action to its most fundamental movements.

A slash or draw-cut to the vulnerable back of the knee or lower leg—a common and effective move.

The buckler's mobility makes it an ideal complement for the agile cut-and-thrust sword.

Clashing bucklers and blades.

Executing a simultaneous hitting parry by the buckler while delivering a countercut was a common means of employing the buckler.

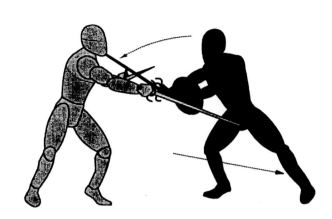

Thrusts can be parried with a sweeping motion, using the face of the buckler. Cuts can be parried by opposing with the buckler's edge.

Parrying outside by dropping back on the left leg and cutting.

It is evident that throughout the 1500s and 1600s, various theories and methods of the cut-and-thrust form were continually in development. They differed noticeably from the newly emerging rapier form.

Stepping in and punching away the attack with a deflecting parry.

With the cut-and-thrust form we begin to see a more conscious effort to break movements down into parry and riposte or a single countering attack of two movement parts. This concept was more valuable when fighting with the rapier and then even more with the small sword.

The larger Renaissance battlefield shield, known as the *target, targe,* or *rondash*, was common at the time, but rarely encountered on the street. Large round or even square shields were worn on the arm and held by straps. They were often concave in shape and made of either wood, iron, or iron-plated wood. A few forms of rondash had built-in gauntlets or mail mittens. Many large shields also included padded armrests. The *rondache* (rondash) was also a type of *targe* used by cavalry and foot swordsmen and for parade. The word *targe* comes from the Norse word *targa* and is the origin of the word *target* (archers once practiced at stuffed dummies with *targes* hanging from them).

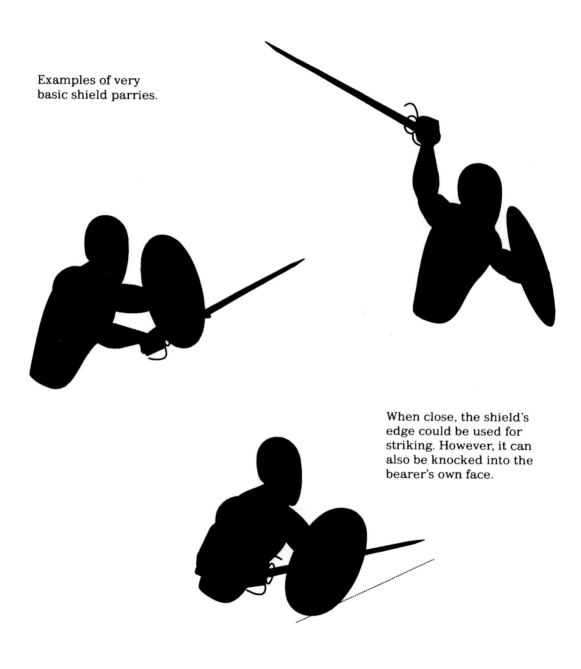

Examples of very basic shield parries.

When close, the shield's edge could be used for striking. However, it can also be knocked into the bearer's own face.

Small by typical medieval shield standards, Renaissance battlefield shields ranged from 22 to 30 inches. Typically, they were made of approximately 3/4-inch wood covered with leather and weighed between one and three pounds. Their use involved a wide range of techniques.

Against cuts, larger shields allowed blows to be taken directly on the front face or on the edge. As they blocked, they also allowed for a simultaneous counterattack with the sword. Although they offered greater defense, they were slower and less maneuverable and not usually carried around town. Against the rapier, such shields can often limit target options.

Instruction in their general use was typically still taught. Their manner of use (such as in the medieval period) was different than that of the smaller, lighter buckler. With larger shields, the leading leg must primarily be that of the shield's side in order to utilize its surface.

It is possible that the absence of large shields in civil quarrels was a factor in the rise of a thrusting sword like the rapier.

SWORD AND DAGGER

Using the dagger with the sword by civilian fighters became a skill of its own, and this combination was increasingly more common than that of the sword and buckler. In the medieval period, the dagger was used primarily only when the sword was lost or broken, or a heavily armored adversary had been taken down. For fighting without a buckler, sword-and-dagger use was a common method and one that led directly to the rapier and dagger.

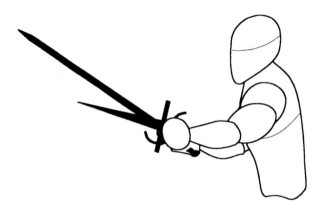

One form of sword-and-dagger guard position has the weapons slightly crossed with the sword on top of the dagger. This allows the dagger to sweep out quickly for a parry or thrust while the sword simultaneously lifts in preparation to parry or countercut.

Perhaps more so than with a rapier, the dagger has a more defensive role with a sword. It is used more to ward off the adversary and prevent him from coming in.

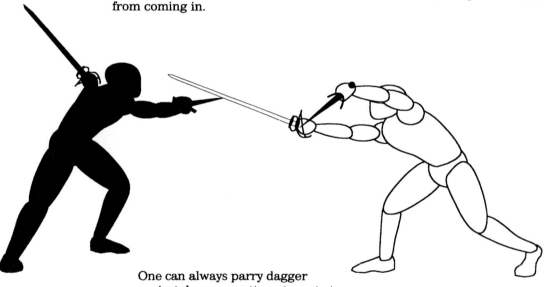

One can always parry dagger against dagger or attempt a cut at the adversary's dagger hand. A buckler may also be used to strike with its edge at a dagger hand.

Daggers commonly used with cut-and-thrust swords were heavier and sturdier than those used with rapiers and were more capable of making both slicing cuts and direct blocks. The dagger is quicker than the sword and in parrying can naturally be moved first. However, its capacity to block more forceful sword blows is limited because of the danger of a misparry. Daggers are better used to deflect in conjunction with the sword and to stab when close in.

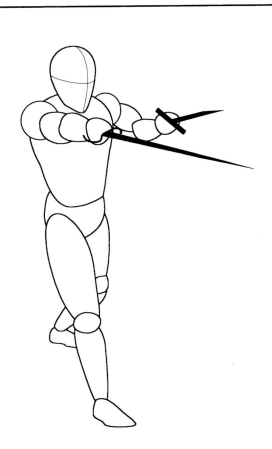

An important factor in delivering effective techniques in swordsmanship (and in most aggressive physical activities or martial skills) is that of tense exhalation. As an attack or move is initiated, the swordsman releases a simultaneous yell or loud exclamation as he forcibly exhales. Doing so has a noticeable effect, both physiologically and psychologically, on the opponent and on the swordsman. This act of tensing and tightening the abdomen and chest adds power to attacks and may improve strikes by helping to regulate breathing as the person exerts. Some suggest that deep, guttural exhalation clears the head and allows for better focusing of strikes. More important, such a burst of energetic, aggressive sound can also startle an opponent (similar to the principle behind an attacking lion's roar). This concept is common and familiar in Asian fighting arts, but certainly not exclusive to them.

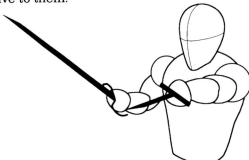

Many of the techniques of the dagger and cut-and-thrust sword have counterparts with those for rapier and dagger and even with those used by heavier medieval swords and shields. Naturally, the origin and development of rapier-and-dagger moves can be more easily traced by studying the use of the sword and dagger.

There are many cultures in which forms of cut-and-thrust swordsmanship developed. Unlike those of the Renaissance period, which evolved from heavier swords used against heavier armor, those other forms (e.g., Chinese, Indonesian, Middle Eastern) tend to stress draw-cuts, more circular or flowing movement, and even curved blades.

One common technique is to step into an attack just as the opponent strikes (as shown). The sword leg steps forward from the rear to close the distance as the dagger simultaneously is lifted to meet and block a high strike while the sword is used to make a low outside cut. As with similar techniques, the concept here it to make one motion of attack and defense timed with the adversary's initial action.

From a position leading with the left (dagger-side) leg (as shown), the swordsman can deliver an effective countercut.

In one motion, the lead leg falls back as the sword is used to strike out at the adversary's oncoming attack, countercutting his sword arm. A well-developed sense of timing and perception is necessary for such action. This technique can also be used for deflecting the opponent's weapon.

To illustrate the sword-and-dagger principles more clearly, most of the techniques are shown against a sword and buckler. They work equally well (if not better) against an attacker wielding only a single sword or a large shield and heavier variety of medieval sword.

An adversary's attack can also be met with crossed weapons performing a simultaneous parry and riposte counter-cut. As the dagger leg steps forward, the sword blade takes the parry while the dagger then drops out from under the parry and cuts across the opponent's wrist or forearm.

Countering across on the attacker's exposed and extended arm while blocking directly with the dagger against a high or mid attack.

An option against a lower attack to the dagger side: a parry down and away (low side) while simultaneously stepping in to deliver a countercut to the weapon arm.

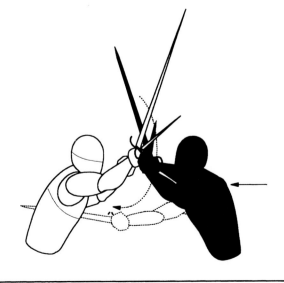

Double parrying offers a solid defense. The dagger is best positioned on top with the sword underneath so it can immediately deliver a cut or forward thrust after the block. However, because the weapons can often become trapped in place, having the sword on top and the dagger below allows the sword to slip off and strike.

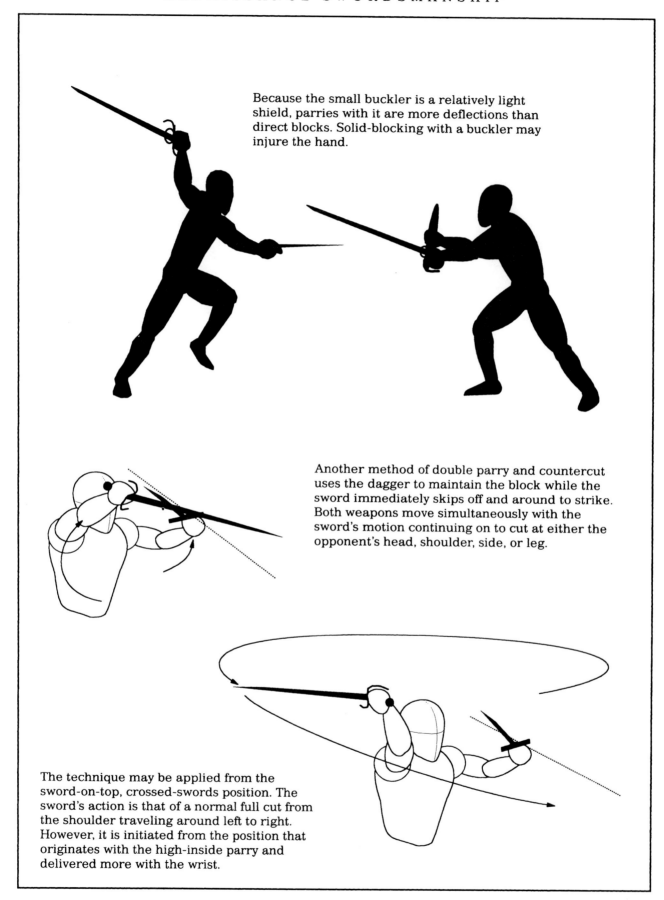

Because the small buckler is a relatively light shield, parries with it are more deflections than direct blocks. Solid-blocking with a buckler may injure the hand.

Another method of double parry and countercut uses the dagger to maintain the block while the sword immediately skips off and around to strike. Both weapons move simultaneously with the sword's motion continuing on to cut at either the opponent's head, shoulder, side, or leg.

The technique may be applied from the sword-on-top, crossed-swords position. The sword's action is that of a normal full cut from the shoulder traveling around left to right. However, it is initiated from the position that originates with the high-inside parry and delivered more with the wrist.

From a position such as that described above, just prior to engaging, the swordsman may execute a stab behind the adversary's shield unexpectedly. The attacker first throws a sword blow to cause his opponent to parry or react by raising his shield or weapon; simultaneously, the swordsman advances his rear (dagger-side) leg and brings a dagger stab around and in. He may employ a variety of strikes or feints to stifle or delay the opponent just prior to the forward step and dagger stab. The technique may also be applied with the sword being used for an initial parry upon closing in.

Even if not for the techniques described in the historical manuals, the fact that swords of the cut-and-thrust form were well established is reason enough to believe that there was a defined method of their use as well.

For combined actions, coordinating the movement of each weapon with proper footwork is crucial. Again, sharpened perception and timing of action are prerequisites. For the most part, it matters not whether the adversary is strong or weak, a novice or an expert. One's own abilities are really the determining factors.

Fundamentally, a fight should be entered into without preconception or design of what specific actions will be. To attack successfully, you must either see an opening or create one. An attack should never be delivered with only a blind chance of hitting. The questions arise then of just how, where, and when to strike. You can wait to counterattack the opponent's attempts, but if he makes none, then you must coerce him into acting. This is achieved by threatening him (e.g., attack, feint, invitation). It is by inducing the adversary to make a mistake or commit himself to an action that his vulnerability can be discerned. It is useful to recall that for every offensive action, there is a defensive counter and vice versa.

At the highest level, fighting is a noncognitive process whereby if we have trained well, we function reflexively on automatic. Emotions of apprehension, doubt, or fear are transcended. Our techniques and movements should be so ingrained as to be free from effort or conscious decision. There is nothing mystical about it. The idea is simply to react and not allow our minds to stop and take time out to think.

An attack can be made in one of four fundamental ways:
1. From inaction—delivering a quick, direct strike when you are relatively still
2. From preparation—delivering a strike after first making some simple preparation such as a feint, bind, beat, or step
3. From combination—delivering any strike after a series of actions (e.g., strikes, beats, feints, made high to low, left to right)
4. From counter—delivering a strike as (or after) the adversary commits his own move
There are no attacks that do not fall into one of these four groups.

Attacks (cuts or thrusts) are naturally made to be unpredictable and thereby overwhelm and outmaneuver the adversary's defense, evasion, or counteractions. Attacks are varied and mixed with regard to angle, target, tempo, and repetition. A compound attack, or an attack to evoke a defensive response that can then be countered, is very useful for this.

Generally, the idea is to seize the initiative and, by attacking or threatening the adversary's openings, cause him to have to react to you. You pressure and exploit his weaknesses and basically take control of his blade (e.g., cuts over, binds it, slides down it, pushes it aside). Often, the sheer fact of slowly advancing at the adversary with your weapon in a threatening position will cause him to react. He must either allow himself to be hit, deliver a counterattack, or beat or parry and attack. The only other option against this is for him to retreat continually. Of course, attempting a continual press can expose your own defense in the process. You must be ever ready to perceive the adversary's response.

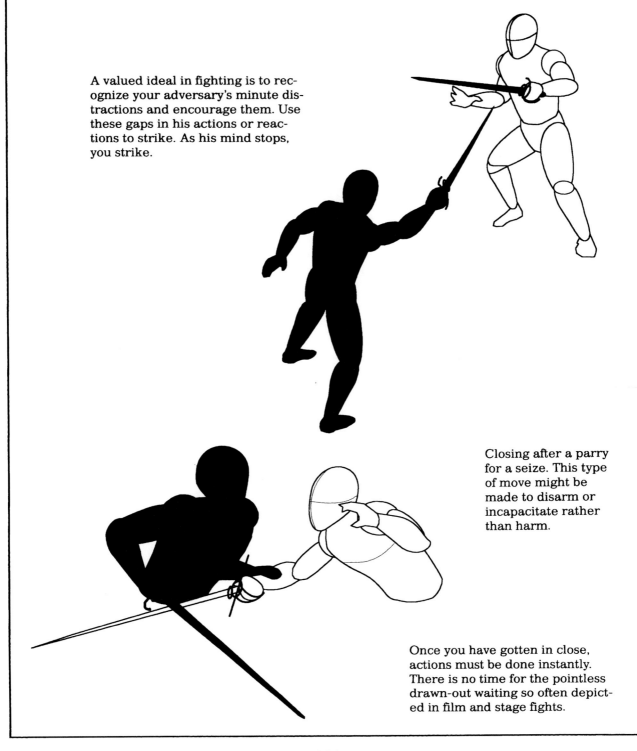

A valued ideal in fighting is to recognize your adversary's minute distractions and encourage them. Use these gaps in his actions or reactions to strike. As his mind stops, you strike.

Closing after a parry for a seize. This type of move might be made to disarm or incapacitate rather than harm.

Once you have gotten in close, actions must be done instantly. There is no time for the pointless drawn-out waiting so often depicted in film and stage fights.

101

Valuable *in-fighting* or close-in techniques are more common with cut-and-thrust swords than with rapiers (because of the longer distance from which the latter fight). Though hard to practice for safety reasons, close-in skills should not be neglected by practitioners today.

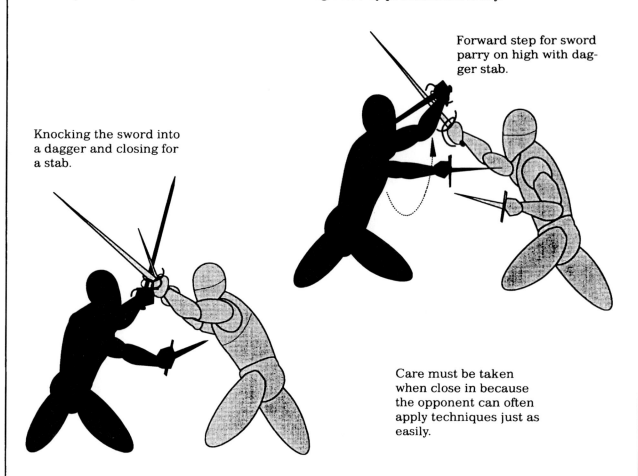

Forward step for sword parry on high with dagger stab.

Knocking the sword into a dagger and closing for a stab.

Care must be taken when close in because the opponent can often apply techniques just as easily.

Grabbing the opponent's wrist, arm, or hilt when he moves or when you can step into him is a common action. As well as positioning him for a thrust or draw-cut, this is often used as a prelude to a pommel or hilt strike, fist punch, disarm attempt, or even a leg sweep. Kicking, pushing, tripping, and body slamming were all used as needed.

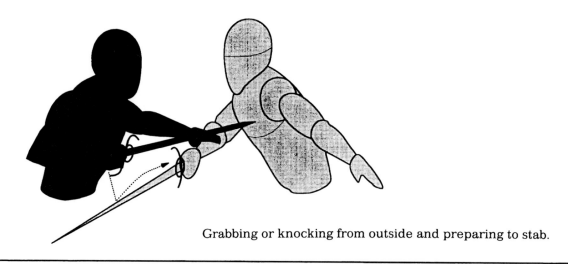

Grabbing or knocking from outside and preparing to stab.

Instead of strength alone, disarms and grabs often use the adversary's own force and motion against him. This can involve shifting stances while lowering and twisting your hips.

At close quarters, leverage can be gained in a number of ways, such as lowering the hips or getting one leg behind the adversary's.

Meeting the attack and grabbing inside (possibly followed by a pommel or hilt blow).

A condition of *contraprinse*— where both combatants move simultaneously to grab each other's weapon, thereby exchanging swords—could sometimes result.

It has been suggested that the majority of theories and systems of unarmed fighting have developed from those first evolved from forms of swordsmanship.

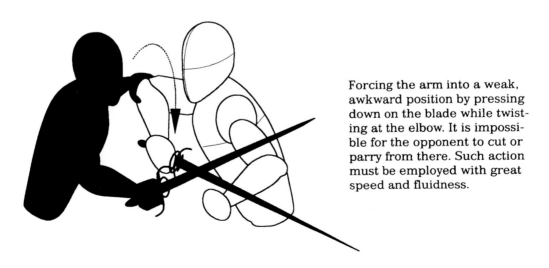

Forcing the arm into a weak, awkward position by pressing down on the blade while twisting at the elbow. It is impossible for the opponent to cut or parry from there. Such action must be employed with great speed and fluidness.

Once the fighters are close in, the cutting edge of the heavier blade has a distinct advantage over the quicker rapier. A buckler can also be used to deliver a solid blow to the face and head.

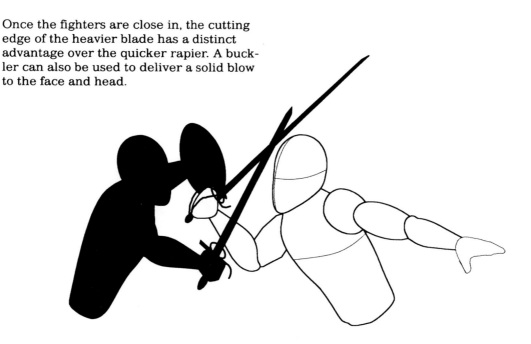

In speculation on Renaissance swordsmanship, you occasionally run across comments that dismiss or repudiate concepts found in some of the historical manuals. There are those modern sport fencers who, being unfamiliar with historical weapons or fighting conditions, will sometimes describe notions of the historical masters as simplistic or misguided. This is unfortunate and ignorant. Modern fencing is a sport, an artificial game. You wonder what the condition of traditional Asian martial arts would be today had they no living followers and instead had to be reconstructed based solely on examination of antique weapons and ancient texts. Such is the condition of a good portion of re-creational sword practice today. The answers lie in intense, serious contact sparring; thorough research; and long-term practice with accurate replicas.

Closing in to grab the wrist while applying blade pressure can twist the opponent's grip into a weak palm-up position. He is left momentarily vulnerable to a draw-cut, pommel strike, or other blow.

Swordsmanship (and most fighting) has been described as a process of juxtapositioning, or maneuvering for advantage. We act, react, and counterreact symbiotically with the adversary. Yet, on a higher level of swordsmanship, it has also been suggested that striking and counterstriking are the same thing. One can learn to move as if alone, and no opponent or target exists as a conscious object.

Although there will always be a stylistic variety among fighters, it exists only within the parameters of the appropriate physical mechanics. When an adversary deviates from this noticeably, because of inexperience or ignorance, it can be exploited. Although any style or technique may have some potential utility (no matter how remote), the idea is to use those that have the greatest potential with the least limitations.

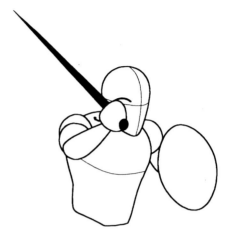

If an opponent holds his weapon cocked and ready on the shoulder to snap out, his range is limited, and he loses parry potential and his attacks are limited to higher angles. Keep your distance and make lower strikes and leg cuts. Throw attacks directly at his grip. Avoid any close-in fighting and use stepping countercuts.

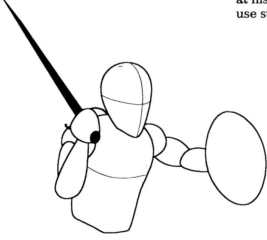

If an opponent holds his weapon too relaxed or with the buckler too extended, his reaction time and counters will be slowed (too much extra movement to move from the ready position). Feints can create openings on your opponent.

If an opponent holds his weapon too vertically, he poses a reduced threat and opens more of his body as a target. He is in neither a warding nor guarding position and loses time and power in both offense and defense. Reaction time and striking power are the worst things to allow to weaken due to improper form.

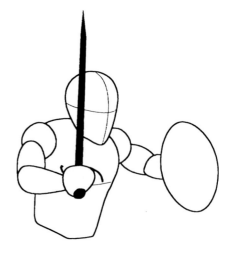

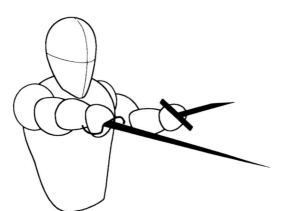

If an opponent hold his weapon too horizontally or overly extended, his ready position is weakened and his range limited. Any cut or move to parry will have to first withdraw to create momentum. The threat of a thrust is already mostly committed and therefor easy to anticipate. Make preparation attacks or beats on your opponent's blade to stifle both his attacks and moves to counter.

Naturally, without intelligent instruction, often the only way we can learn is when another fighter, through the act of besting us, reveals the error of our misconceptions. *Although there are only a few ways to properly handle a weapon for defense or offense, there are seemingly innumerable ways to mishandle one.*

RAPIER AGAINST CUT-AND-THRUST SWORD

Among the many possible ways to fight against the rapier, a cut-and-thrust swordsman might attempt to beat aside the lighter blade, deflecting its dangerous tip off line, and then recover with a slashing motion or stab. It is also possible to parry with a dagger or buckler and deliver a cut that has already been raised.

It is no wonder that civilian sword-and-dagger fighting was perhaps more prominent with the rapier method than with the cut-and-thrust sword. It is generally harder to block a sword cut with a dagger and parry a rapier thrust with a slower sword. A typical defense in either case is to sidestep an attack, letting it pass or slip by. In counterattacking this way, circular movement can be used against linear movement. To defend against heavier cuts and beats, the rapier fighters might also cross-parry with both sword and dagger.

Intentionally extending a weapon to evoke a reaction that could then be countered was at one time known as "giving the blade."

There is not a clear distinction between the blade shapes or fighting methods of many early rapiers and those of the cut-and-thrust variety. This has been the cause of a good deal of error in reconstructing both styles.

Stopping the attack by a quicker preemptive thrust into it (called a *stop thrust* or *stop hit*).

It is possible against a cut-and-thrust sword for a rapier fighter to avoid any direct cuts and dart in with thrusts when the opening presents itself. The movement of the opponent's slower blade in rising to cut or lowering to block or stab creates the opportunity. Although most rapiers were indeed capable of blocking cuts directly, there was always the danger of their being broken by the heavier weapon or having the opponent close in to draw-cut.

In England especially, the rapier began to supplant the native cut-and-thrust form for personal fighting. It grew first in popularity among the gentry and then among the common folk.

An attack to the hand, often an easy target.

Although the use of armored gripping gauntlets was known in civilian fights, the rarity of using the free hand for defense in cut-and-thrust sword action is obvious. Doing so would offer little protection and expose the hand and arm to blows or grappling moves. Only the lighter rapier with its lack of cutting ability made full use of the free hand possible.

Trapping the blade with a wrist (or hilt) grab by stepping in and parrying out. This can be followed up with a strike, draw-cut, pommel blow, or disarm. This can also be applied parrying to the outside. Against a rapier, the blade itself can often be grabbed.

The danger for the cut-and-thrust swordsman is in being outmaneuvered and outtimed by the rapier fighter's range and faster counterthrust attack. The rapier fighter must avoid being drawn in where his speed and range are neutralized and a cutting blade has the advantage. Although a minor thrust may be merely annoying, a minor cutting blow can be far more serious and debilitating.

A counterthrust stab at a primary target: the face.

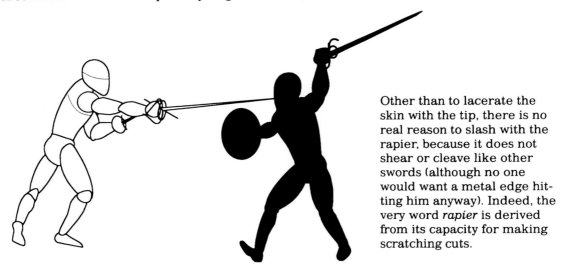

Other than to lacerate the skin with the tip, there is no real reason to slash with the rapier, because it does not shear or cleave like other swords (although no one would want a metal edge hitting him anyway). Indeed, the very word *rapier* is derived from its capacity for making scratching cuts.

A solid rapier thrust could even pierce clean through the head.

A fast, light cut to the face or head (*stromazione* or *stramazone*) was often used to distract and harass the adversary. This often opened the adversary to a more lethal thrust. Light cuts to the hand and limb joints are also possible, depending on the blade. It is also far too easy to unintentionally hit flat with the rapier's thinner blade.

It is interesting to note that despite the great speed of cuts in sport saber fencing today, under the rules thrusts still take precedence over cuts in scoring touches.

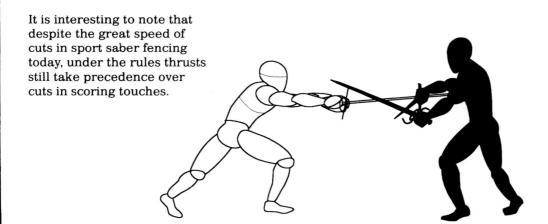

The great reach advantage of a thrusting sword on the lunge. Such thrusts could also be made while stepping back with the rear leg.

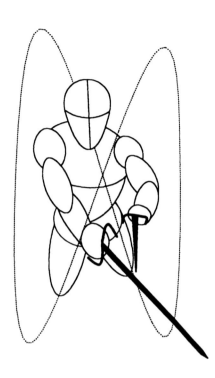

One technique against the rapier is to make repeated "figure eight" cuts while moving in. Quick, slashing motions combined with a forward rush can sometimes prevent a rapier thrust and force its bearer on the defensive. This is quite distinct from the useless twirling a sword from the wrist so often seen in movies and copied by novices.

It must be pointed out that not only was single combat or a personal duel different from battlefield fighting, but also from chance encounters with highwaymen or back-alley cutthroats. Unlike with the rapier, practice with the sword seems to have reflected more of this.

In any practice sparring, judgments must be made and criteria established to acknowledge what blows or touches will be considered hits or not. Hits must then be defined as to whether they are killing blows, disabling wounds, or incapacitating dismemberments. These standards and judgments are somewhat subjective matters for the participants, but developing them must be based on objective understanding of the power of cuts and thrusts.

Stepping in with a sword parry, followed by a dagger slash on the arm.

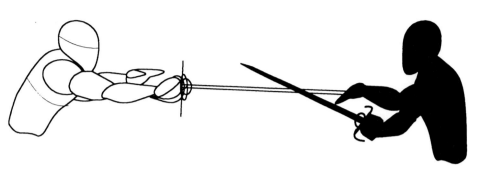

The full-arm extension attack of a rapier on the often exposed free hand.

In the true spirit of the Renaissance, the study of arms was the subject of greater investigation and found greater respect than ever before in Europe. However, for various reasons, the profession of instructor of fence or master at arms was usually seen as lowly and even ignoble (particularly in England).

A stop-cut of a rapier by slashing the wrist.

Beating aside a rapier thrust and delivering a slice or draw-cut.

In private (and usually unlawful) duels, combatants were known to secretly wear mail or hard leather under their shirts as a defense against a blade piercing their skin. Against a rapier, mail could often prevent full penetration. As a result, it was sometimes customary to duel shirtless.

Unlike with earlier swords where judicial or personal duels and even streetfights might end with just a small cut or continue with each fighter hacking and beating the other's blade (thereby wearing each other out), the rapier changed things. It added a much higher risk of serious wounds because of its thrust (the incident of simultaneous kills seems to have been quite high). One could also not engage any longer in a "manly brawl" with simply dulled versions. With the rapier, it was just too easy to stick someone lethally and not so easy to make simpler body cuts or smaller wounds that might justify ending a scuffle. In single combat, more so than on the crowded battlefield, personal skill is the overriding factor.

An example of one of the numerous ways of trapping with the guard by twisting the hilt against the adversary's blade. Against a rapier, it is possible to break the blade this way. Some hilt designs were better at this than others. When necessary, the guards on the hilt can indeed be used for beating or even direct blocking.

Many masters of the art supposedly professed to having some special technique or secret attack (*botta segreta*) that they revealed to only a close few. One such secret might have been a *botte de paysan*, a two-handed stab made by grabbing your blade near the middle with the free hand and closing in to knock aside an opponent's weapon, thus shortening the distance and increasing the force of beat. Such techniques were not so much "secret" as perhaps simply favored, yet sparingly taught.

Fighting is not exclusively a matter of either pressing the attack forward or falling back from it. Rather, both are to be applied as necessary, depending upon the nature of the adversary's fight.

Passato sotto
(or *botte de nuit*).

When we consider the scope and magnitude of the revolutions in military technology and methodology that swept Europe in the centuries from the Dark Ages to the Industrial Age, it is no wonder that the traditions of true sword fighting did not prevail. The sociological and technological conditions were too different from those of the Asian countries that were able to maintain and preserve their medieval fighting arts virtually intact. In Europe, the ascendancy of the pistol in dueling and of firearms and cannon in warfare reduced swordsmanship (with the possible exception of some forms of cavalry) to virtual obsolescence.

Ducking below
and attacking on
the knee with a
rapier thrust.

The reader is advised not to try and draw too distinctive a line between the cut-and-thrust and rapier methods. Although the two weapon forms are indeed separate, many concepts and techniques (other than cuts) cross over, just as they did in the transition from the medieval to the cut-and-thrust style. The idea is to not treat any weapon's use as strictly black and white. Although most cut-and-thrust swords can be used in a rapier-like manner, no true rapier can be used like a cut-and-thrust sword. As the characteristics of fighting with the new rapier blades began to establish themselves, those techniques of the cut-and-thrust method that were inappropriate or unnecessary were gradually discontinued.

In typical Renaissance fashion, the new methods and theories of rapier fighting began to stress inquiry, analysis, and empiricism over raw talent, improvisation, and force. There can be no doubt that swordsmen of the period were experimenting with different sword blade forms and their corresponding techniques. There were many different notions, some of them contradictory, about what worked best and why. Eventually, the cut-and-thrust variety of Renaissance sword blade fell out of general use. As a personal sword, it was replaced by the more vicious and elegant rapier, and on the battlefield it was eclipsed by the curved saber (more suitable for the new cavalry armies).

Question: What is the best weapon?
Answer: The one you win with!

In re-creating historical fencing, we should keep in mind that civilian swordsmen and theorists of the age who still practiced the cut-and-thrust style were really only beginning to work out the mechanics and tactics of using the thrusting rapier sword for self-defense. By the time the method did become fully established, the small-sword form was already appearing.

THE CUT-AND-THRUST SWORD AGAINST THE TWO-HANDED SWORD

Facing a two-handed sword was always a possibility whether on the battlefield or elsewhere. Going up against its unique characteristics is something that should be familiar to any swordsmen. Although fighting one can be intimidating, by relying on the fundamental principles of swordsmanship, it can be overcome, without great difficulty. All that is different about fighting a two-hander or a great sword is adjusting to the different timing and distance. The weapon's length and slower recovery must be exploited.

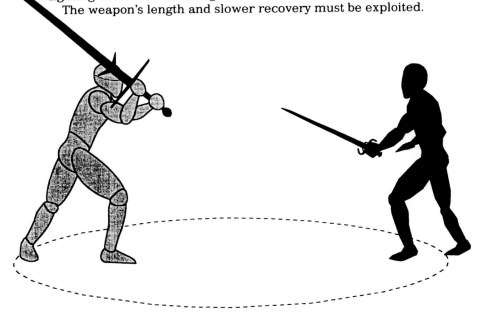

Once stepping into the range of the longer weapon, it must be covered quickly and safely. There is very little room for mistakes.

Because of the two-hander's weight and inertia, the same stances, guards, or assorted techniques are not used in the same way as those for lighter one-handed blades. Two-handers are principally used with the seven basic cuts and a straight thrust; for defense, their owners rely mostly on their length and a few basic parries. The footwork used with a two-hander consists typically of passes, traverses, and cross-stepping—all of which a cut-and-thrust sword fighter should try to outmaneuver.

Because of its weight, the two-hander is seldom held in a middle guard or low-forward guard. When facing a lighter sword, the two-hander's user cannot afford to have his sword being bound up and caught taking too long to ready his blows.

Stepping in preemptively.

Usually the two-handed sword is held close to the shoulder and in either a high or a low guard. Strikes are made with wider movements of the elbow and hilt in bringing the tip around. Most of its blocks are done overhanded with the pommel up. The swordsman uses the momentum from the cut to recover and return the blade along another line of attack. It is this action that a lighter sword can use to advantage, because the two-hander cannot be used to "sword fight" in the same manner as the lighter blade, nor can it match the latter's action.

The two-handed sword's effectiveness lies in its reach and power. It can be used to deliver cuts in wide, sweeping arcs and can be surprisingly agile. The techniques for the two-hander are similar to those for other swords; the difference lies in the cumbersome style that makes the two-hander relatively slower and less manageable. However, it makes up for this in the strength of its blows and the devastating power of its cuts.

Because of a two-handed sword's forceful blows, directly blocking its strikes is not easy. Attempting to block a two-hander can overpower a parry and disrupt recovery. The key to fighting such a large weapon is in voiding and traversing. By outtiming the blade's swings, you can either evade them completely and countercut or allow them to pass by and follow up with a stepping-in strike.

When using the sword and buckler or sword and dagger, you should endeavor to tie the weapon up and not allow it to utilize its wider, stronger cutting arc. The two-hander is by nature a very offensive weapon, and a fighter can gain an advantage by forcing his opponent to go on the defensive with it, where it is less versatile. This can be done by closing and sticking.

Closing in to strike in-time with the two-hander's attack.

The two-hander can also be gripped at the ricasso and the length quickly shortened. You must take caution against this and against the two-hander's long, spear-like, horizontal thrusts. Again, deflecting and outstepping, rather than directly opposing, can neutralize the two-handed sword's advantages. The wielder of a two-hander can be made to overextend himself in throwing cuts and swings while the swordsman remains outside of range and looks for the opportunity to close just prior to or just after a strike is delivered.

By not fighting in the two-hander's preferred range, you can tie it up and outfight it by closing in. Once you are closer, the advantage lies with the shorter, quicker blade. You can deliver thrusts up under the two-handed user's guard or make slashes on his exposed forearms. However, the wielder of the two-hander is not helpless when close in. He can make dangerous blows with the weapon's large pommel or its hilt, or parries with its longer handle. Those weapons with flukes on the ricasso can be used to maintain range while blocking or even to strike with.

Rushing in and pressing the blade against the exposed forearms before the blow can be committed.

The two-handed sword was not intended as much for fighting against sword and buckler or sword and dagger as for fighting pole arms or other two-handed swords. Training in using it against more common swords made sense for Renaissance swordsmen, and experience with it is advisable for practitioners today.

Rushing in with a thrust in between the forearms.

THE CUT-AND-THRUST SWORD AGAINST POLE ARMS

Using pole weapons or pole-arms (e.g., spears, glaives, bills, halberds, quarter staffs) is an art unto itself. Encountering adversaries armed with such weapons was a distinct possibility on the battlefield or elsewhere. The use of pole-arms was taught in the schools alongside that of swords and other weapons. Though incidental to the sword, pole-arms were still respected and highly effective implements used for thrusting, cutting, thrusting and cutting, and other tasks. Defense against them was typically part of weapon study. Although they cannot be covered in depth here, fundamentals of their use against the cut-and-thrust sword must be discussed.

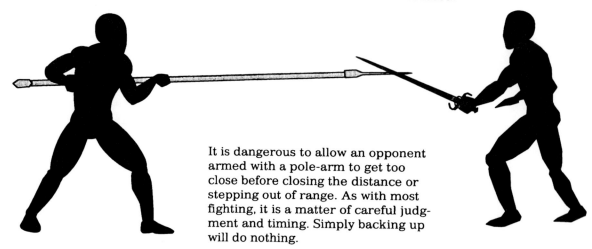

It is dangerous to allow an opponent armed with a pole-arm to get too close before closing the distance or stepping out of range. As with most fighting, it is a matter of careful judgment and timing. Simply backing up will do nothing.

For the most part, pole-arms are either thrusting, striking, or thrusting-and-striking weapons. Their chief advantage is range, for both offense and defense. However, their speed, force, and deceptiveness should not be underestimated. The attacks, parries, and footwork used with a pole weapon are essentially the same as those used with a sword.

Defense with a pole weapon relies on opposition blocks and deflecting parries within the same four areas as a sword (inside high, outside high, inside low, outside low). Attacks come in the form of straight and angulating thrusts and straight and crossing blows. Additionally, you can fight with or against pole weapons by using the same concepts of feints, beats, disengages, glides, grabs, etc. The major difference is one of reach and timing: you must alter the distance and movement that you would use when fighting against a sword. The vulnerable areas of an opponent armed with a pole weapon are primarily the hands and arms, and this is often overlooked in most sparring. Even a simple blow on a hand can render the opponent helpless. Because the pole-arm is a two-handed weapon, a strike on the arm or hand can disable the adversary far more easily than if he was using another weapon.

A middle parry to the inside. It is crucial to attempt to close and/or grab after a solid parry (not a deflect or beat) has been made.

The brutal speed of a pole weapon's thrust and its formidable capability to feint and disengage are often underestimated. This is ruinous. A skillful practitioner (although reasonably uncommon) can be as effective, and sometimes more so, than even an expert swordsman.

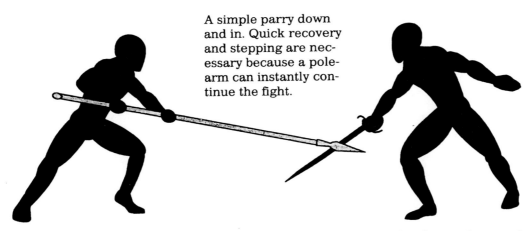

A simple parry down and in. Quick recovery and stepping are necessary because a pole-arm can instantly continue the fight.

Pole weapons can be used to make wide, sweeping strikes and circular thrusts that are deceptive in their difficulty of being intercepted or blocked. Opponents with pole weapons can often recover from misses and foiled attacks in safety and immediately renew their attempts. The ability of an opponent to easily alter the pole weapon's range by shifting and sliding the grip is one more of the weapon's assets. Another lies in the unpredictability of its quickly moving tip (although this varies with the type of blade or point it may have). Those pole-arms with hooked or beaked blade heads offer additional problems as well as opportunities. These blades can be used to trap, pull, push, and hook a sword with considerable force. Of course, this can work both ways; a pole-arm may be locked and forced down or held long enough to be grabbed and closed in on. Also, the possibility that a pole-arm fighter may let go of his weapon with one or both hands and draw a dagger or short sword must not be overlooked. A swordsman ignorantly rushing in can fall victim to this tactic.

The key to defeating an opponent armed with a pole weapon is getting past the weapon's point. This is not easy. However, once achieved, a pass, step, or lunge can be delivered against either the opponent's arm (often the closest target), body, or head. The weakness of a pole-arm is in its propensity to be tied up and trapped once a swordsman has closed past its tip. The pole user is typically forced to pull the shaft back in defense, thereby moving the point off line. With the point out of the way and the swordsman close, the fight takes on a different character. The pole-arm fighter must retreat to a safer range or invoke the reverse end of the shaft.

Application of voids and passes is less useful when fighting opponents armed with pole-arms, once again because of the weapon's reach. However, the pole-arm fighter may himself employ these techniques effectively, especially with reverse strikes using the back end.

Parrying high inside and grabbing with a step or pass.

Remember that a pole weapon has two ends and a middle, all of which can be used to strike or parry. However, remember also that the motion of changing from one end to the other can create a minute but exploitable gap for you to counterattack. Additionally, once you have closed on the adversary, agile and speedy use of a sword can be decisive.

A free hand, by being quicker and having the ability to grasp, can be more effective against a pole weapon than either a buckler or dagger. The dagger cannot be used to trap a shaft with much effectiveness and is too short to easily harm the opponent. As well, defending with a buckler is of minimal value where trapping and grabbing are more important.

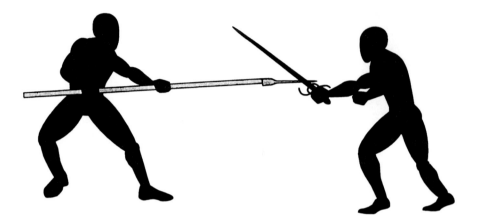

At a certain range, the opportunity to bind or deflect the pole-arm must be weighed against the often greater chance of being stabbed by it in return.

Basic techniques against a pole-arm include using a middle stance and readying against an attack. As a pole-arm comes in, it must be judged carefully and met in order to parry and step in. Continuing on, the blade can glide along the shaft, thereby keeping pressure on the pole-arm user and closing the striking range. The initial parry and closure of the shaft is not easy because its bearer often feints or disengages. All the while, he will try to keep the pole-arm at its optimal range.

Parry down and out, to be followed with a pass. From here, you can initiate a grab or attack by a simple thrust or even make a pivoting spin to bring the blade from around the back.

Once you have closed with your opponent, you may employ an immediate grab to seize the shaft or even use a dagger with the second hand. You may even use the foot or shin to kick or step on the pole. Having grabbed hold of the pole, you may force or maneuver it out of the way, while making a cut or stab. You can even employ it in defense should the adversary let go with one hand and draw a second weapon. Grabbing or trapping the shaft ties it up and prevents the adversary from using the reverse end with which to strike. When grabbing the shaft, it is vital to lower your hips and knees and stiffen your arm to gain leverage. In this way, you can put your body weight behind the seizure and add strength to the hold.

Although this is less common with heavier pole-arms, pole-arm users can easily reverse the shaft in order to strike with the opposite end. This is done in the familiar "staff fighting" manner and allows for fast, strong, deceptive blows. However, again, the hands and arms are far more vulnerable to swords than most martial arts and fighting displays would have you believe.

Another effective technique to be wary of is "slipping," or the slip thrust. To make an even quicker attack, pole-arm users may throw the shaft out in a one-handed thrust, slipping it through the first hand's grip. Although this technique has less force, it can significantly alter the range of the attack. It can leave the pole-arm vulnerable on the recovery, should it fail. The pole-arm user's lower legs can be especially vulnerable once a shield user has closed in on them.

Turning to the outside (right) for a down-and-out parry and seize.

On the other hand, against pole weapons the shield or targe does have an advantage: its larger area can be used to deflect or knock a pole-arm when closing in. In so doing, the swordsman must be alert for high feints, followed by low blows to the shins and knees. Reverse low feints, followed by high strikes, are also dangerous. Once close in, a larger shield can be used to block almost all strikes by a pole-arm.

The attack may be beaten or parried down and out, or scooped up, depending on its angle. Either way, the goal is to rapidly close in to attack or grab and strike. Should the adversary break free or maneuver out of the way, you must quickly recover into a strong, flexible middle-guard position. Above all, you must force the distance to the sword's advantage and not try to fight to the pole-arm's reach.

Against rapiers, a pole-arm can negate their reach and agility, while exploiting their weaker parrying capacity. The rapier's lack of cutting power is also a major hindrance here. The rapier must rely on its length and angulation to defend, close quickly, and get in a lethal thrust. Fighting a pole-arm with a rapier is even more challenging than with a sword.

Just as when fighting any weapon, there are no hard-and-fast rules for victory when fighting against pole-arms. There are, however, discernible principles that can be effective if they are learned well and practiced frequently. Pole-arms are ancient weapons that exist in endless forms in most cultures. No sword skill or training is complete without reference to them. This was the case even for swordsmen of the Renaissance.

As a form of self-defense and battlefield utility, methods of swordsmanship were almost always available in printed form throughout the Renaissance (for those who could read and afford them). Six of the most influential and widely known of these are di Grassi's *His True Arte of Defense* (1594), Vincentio Saviolo's *His Practice in Two Books* (1595), George Silver's *Paradoxes of Defense* (1599), Marozzo's *Il Duello* of 1517, Agrippa's *Treatise* of 1553, and the highly influential work of Ridolfo Capo Ferro in 1610. (For a list of books available during this period, see the suggested reading list in the back of the book.)

Many of these works were illustrated and incorporated techniques of grappling and unarmed fighting as well. Although the authors often disagreed or contradicted one another and showed national bias, the various approaches and levels of study among them reveal an evolving distinction between the cut-and-thrust and rapier forms. Schools of fence (*salles d'armes*) prospered throughout most of Western Europe when men of all classes and stations recognized that the sword was the great equalizer in personal combat.

The works of the classical fencing masters make the most sense when we determine whether they are using military cut-and-thrust swords or civilian rapiers. In many of these works, we see only the beginnings of the rapier method—a method that becomes clearer when we consider the kind of sword they were using it against originally (i.e., the cut-and-thrust varieties). It is really only in later works that they deal with a more developed form of rapier-versus-rapier fighting.

The etchings, drawings, and woodcuts of the blades in many period illustrations are not precise. There is ambiguity in whether the figures are using forms of rapiers or even slim cut-and-thrust swords. The artwork is highly stylized and often shows a distorted perspective and scale. It also likely reflects the personal style and form of the author rather than any generalized techniques. Often, the figures are caught in a vague pose that makes it unclear whether it is a strike or parry. Also a good number of illustrations of arms and armor available are actually 19th-century, not Renaissance, works and therefore of questionable accuracy.

The figures are often shown caught in the act of either parrying or making a swing, but it is not always easy to determine which, even with the help of a text. These drawings cannot be taken literally. It takes an experienced eye to determine what actions might have preceded or followed here. Often the subtleties of movement or form were assumed by the author and so were left out. Regardless of inaccuracies with period art, it is the best source we have and directs modern enthusiasts to investigate on their own.

In keeping with the enlightened and exploratory spirit of the age, the new rapier techniques were innovations by practitioners and theorists of the Renaissance. These ideas were later carried further by adherents of the small sword and, finally, by modern fencers who have elevated their small-sword sport version almost to a science.

In many of these drawings, you can see techniques that have modern fencing equivalents (e.g., lunges, stances, parries, disengages). In others, the actions are unique to the weapons and conditions of Renaissance fighting.

The phrase "traditional European swordsmanship" has little meaning, or at least not in the same sense that "traditional Asian fighting arts" does. There are no surviving schools of established teachings, and we have only a collection of reconstructed theories as our method. This is enough, however, and it is quite understandable considering the vast changes and revolution in military technology that European civilization underwent in just the past 600 years. It is sad that despite the quantity of material published in Europe on swordsmanship, so much of it still remains obscure and underappreciated. This is ironic considering the wealth of information currently available on once "secret" Asian fighting arts.

A pass and thrust while grabbing (from Capo Ferro, 1610).

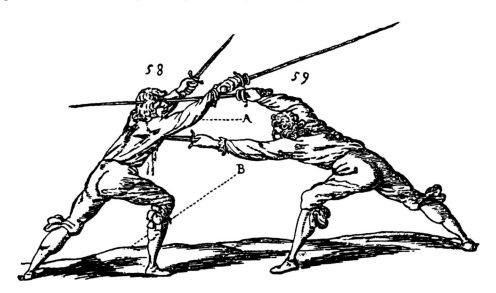

A double attack after parry (from Alfieri, 1640).

A killing thrust by passing and opposition with the free hand (from Fabris, 1606).

German rapier school, circa 1600. Note the disarms occurring in the background.

German rapier instruction, early 1600s.

Cut-and-thrust sword practice (from Joachim Meyer, circa 1600).

Unlike what passes for sword fights in the movies, where the fighters do everything *but* try to stab or cut one another, both rapier and cut-and-thrust sword fights are usually far less animated and much more cautious. For dramatic effect, movies and staged fights must exaggerate both the importance and the frequency of blade-to-blade contact, showing combatants basically hacking at each other's swords and sometimes even making every attempt to place their own sword in the direct path of the other. Usually they can be seen making extrawide strokes and broad, exaggerated parries. In poorer fight scenes, you can even tell that, if the performer were to just lift his sword out of the way, the opponent would cut only air and miss by two feet or more. The fighters are shown making swing after swing and delivering blow after blow without ever moving to feint or fake the opponent. The weapons used for film and stage are usually inaccurate designs, double-weight versions that distort true performance or sometimes flimsy, half-weight versions or even aluminum to increase the actors' speed.

Movie fights are also notorious for displaying any opportunity to grab, push, pull, and knock the opponent, thereby missing just about every chance to do what they are supposed to be doing with the weapon—kill the other person. Take a good, close look at most movies, and it becomes clear that they are less interested in connecting with attacks than in following their programmed moves. Often, even in the best choreographed (or "telegraphed") fights, you can even catch the pauses as fighters freeze their actions right until their opponent is ready. The fights frequently appear overly rehearsed and dance-like.

To increase the action and quicken the pace, choreographers and fight directors resort to a traditional theatrical fighting with its many operatic slapsticks and clichés. Although fighters historically relied on anything to win, most instances of knees in the groin, elbows in the face, dramatic pauses for dialog, and kicks to the backside are pure fiction. Most such moves would get you killed very quickly. Faced with this, fight directors and performers wish to avoid the two most likely possibilities: that the fight be very quick and brutal because one fighter is totally outclassed and quickly killed, or that it be drawn out and slow as neither party acts for quite some time. Skilled, experienced fighters are patient and cautious, even when intense. Although a fight might seem to be in limbo because of a lack of quick movement, much of the action is too subtle or quick to be of interest to most movie fight choreographers. The general public, ignorant of the subtle complexities of swordsmanship, doesn't know any better and merely wishes entertainment in sword fights.

Even when done quite well, choreographed swordplay is still rarely more than a fantasized version of the real thing. It is about following a prescribed pattern, not moving freely; safety rather than contact is paramount. There are fundamental differences between sparring and theatrical fighting. Training exclusively in stage combat or choreographed fighting builds a noticeably distorted and artificial sense of distance, timing, and rhythm. The theories of modern theatrical combat, though fine for the structured scenes of film and stage, just do not appropriately prepare fighters for contact sparring. For practitioners seeking something more martial, they must look instead to forms of open contact sparring.

Despite the developments of modern sport versions, it's foolish to think that after a few decades of playing at swords we can replicate the skill and form of those who fought for real to defend their very lives. All we can hope to do is approximate them closely.

It is important to fully appreciate just how brutal a real sword duel was in comparison to the rule-bound, safety-conscious martial-sport versions of today. Thousands of young men were slain during the eras of violent quarrels and lethal duels. To practice a simulated form of historical fencing, limitations and regulations are certainly necessary. However, practitioners should realize that making fencing moves and safe touches is substantially different from the reality of two people *doing everything they can to stick each other with a sharp piece of metal*. Keeping this uppermost in mind helps us better appreciate the origin of those very concepts and techniques that we so enjoy today.

It is difficult to explain how so much of swordsmanship just cannot be learned from books or even passed on verbally. It must be acquired personally, subjectively, firsthand. It has been said that misunderstanding the basic mechanics of a weapon is the surest way of deluding yourself into misapplying techniques or inventing invalid ones. Enthusiasts who sincerely seek skill must strive to ever examine their preconceptions even at the risk of bruising their egos. Acquiring knowledge (skill) often means risking your self-esteem and reexamining preconceptions. As with almost all the techniques and concepts described in this book, knowing is only half of the answer; you must also do—and that can be achieved only through committed, long-term practice.

As when using any sword, skill is partly a matter of physical conditioning, technical proficiency, and mental development (i.e., perception of distance, timing, and intention). Beyond mere technique there is an infinite number of tactical combinations that require a proper understanding of preparation and movement. This experience comes about only through practice and fighting. Skill with the sword cannot be obtained by merely reading, theorizing, or fantasizing; skill is gained only by training hard and sparring.

To follow the "way of the sword" earnestly and to be a true warrior, it is not necessary to go to war or kill or be violent, but only to practice diligently and humanely with a martial spirit.

THE TREE OF SWORDSMANSHIP DEVELOPMENT

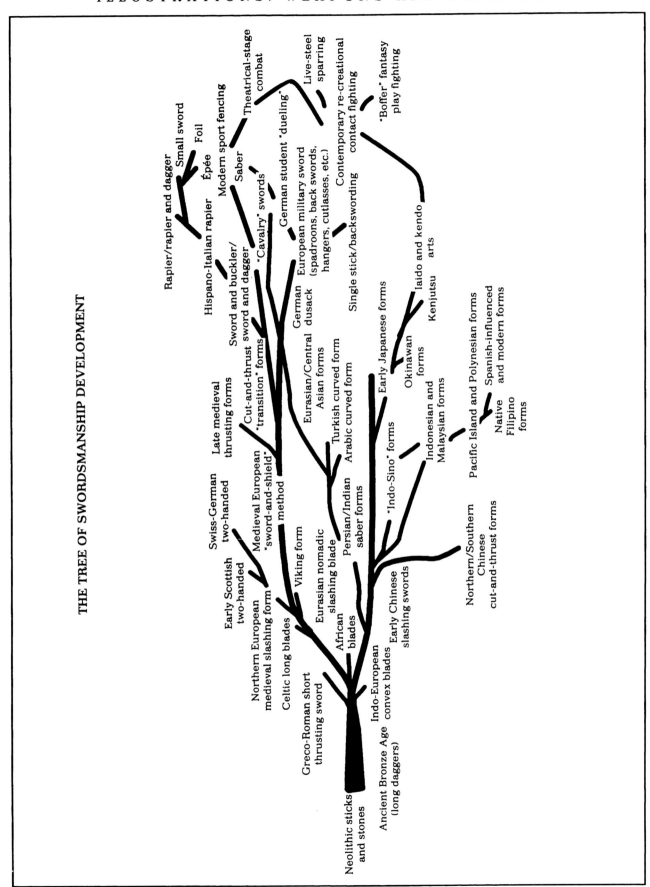

Epilogue

The history of the sword has often been called the history of humanity. No other weapon in the world has the heritage of, nor is as revered as, the hilted blade. Indeed, when we consider how ubiquitous swords are on flags, emblems, signs, and statues, it is rather surprising that its tradition has not been kept more alive in the West.

Although it is often forgotten, the influence of the sword can still be felt in everyday life. For example, in many countries it is customary to drive on the left because people once walked on the left. They did this because most of them were right-handed and they would draw their swords to the right and needed the space. Men's coats are buttoned left over right so that a gentleman could unbutton it with the free left hand while he was engaged in a duel. For similar reasons, a gentleman escorts a lady on his right arm, keeping both his sword arm free and his weapon out of her way. These customs come down to us in the same manner as those for shaking right hands (thought to originally have been a Germanic custom of showing that the weapon hand was empty) or the military salute (a remainder from armored knights lifting their visors to identify themselves). Even the phrase *rapier wit* can now have deeper meaning.

In pursuing historical swordsmanship today, whether as personal martial art or organized martial sport, you must realize certain abstract fundamentals. Swordsmanship is learned like most any other martial art: individual techniques are practiced until the student becomes proficient. All the while, students must pay close attention to their correct performance until combinations of such can be easily applied.

But unlike during other physical activities in which the movements are either prearranged or random, such as dancing, the choice of technique in battle depends on an opponent's actions in the situation. This necessitates the development of heightened perception and spontaneous, unconscious reactions to control the combat distance and the timing of moves. This development is achieved through repetition of techniques until they become internalized and reflexive; thus no time is wasted in having to think about actions, and nothing is given away to the opponent. We must hone our reflexes through endless drills and sparring. In a fight the initiative for an attack may be of one's own timing or prompted by the opponent. Either way, it can never be entirely analytical. In a fraction of a second, there is simply no time for the "observe-orient-decide-act" process to take place. But to develop this intuitive aspect of sword use (or any weapon) requires more than technical skill and physical conditioning. It requires the subtler and more complex psychological factors that are gained only through serious sparring. Only sparring over the long term reveals to us our inadequacies and deficiencies and teaches us tactics. Classroom drills and practice are good, but real ability can only be gained through fighting.

Although learning is mostly a conscious, cognitive process, developing true skill involves a lack of thought and a "blank mind." Thus, you must think to learn and train, but later consciousness of your actions will be "forgotten" and replaced with an "empty" attitude. Learning is often a paradox in this sense. It takes a conscious, thoughtful effort (and will) to train and practice until what is learned is forgotten in the mind but not the body. As well, the more you learn the more you realize your previous ignorance.

It is well known that a beginner's movements and actions are very natural and raw at first. They are untainted by learning (whether correct or incorrect). They can be awkward and unrefined, but still unpredictable and fluid. As you later learn the actual techniques, you can become stiff and hesitant. As your mind

stops to ponder what your body is trying to do, you become vulnerable to those who perceive this hesitation. It is no secret that as this process continues and you develop the coordination and skills to execute proper movements, your actions will become reflexive and natural. This continues until the nature of the sword is unconscious and fluid once again. You return to the mind-set of a beginner, and the "circle of learning" closes. There is nothing mystical about all this (nor a need to make it so), only wonderment when you realize it.

The practice of swordsmanship is a continual process of refinement. You never truly master it; you just go further along. People enter the study at different levels, and some may progress quickly. Others may get sidetracked or wander off course. To begin, you bring only what you have within yourself, mentally and physically, and so it is like looking in a mirror, which honestly reflects only what is brought before it—in all its glory and flaws.

In the long run, what swordsmanship offers, other than the physical benefits of exercise and stress relief, is a change in the character of the person wielding the blade. The requirements of self-discipline, commitment, perseverance, and patience transfer outside of the art. So too is the need for self-control and focus, mental and physical. At the highest level, the development of perception, insight, and intuition can eventually begin to alter one's perspective on life. As with any martial art that is practiced with sincerity and commitment, true swordsmanship cannot be taught—it must be self-learned. It has as its goal the defeat of the ego, the self. Few ever realize that this is the constant and ultimate opponent to be overcome.

Although most practitioners today have had to learn through self-discovery and research, no one can really say, "I am a self-taught swordsman," unless he has lived alone on another planet. We all learn something, whether we realize it or not, from every book we've read or film we've seen that features sword fighting. We also learn something about ourselves every time we spar or practice with someone else. Added to this, we may have been taught traditional collegiate fencing, Asian sword styles, or the practices of some historical fantasy organization. But for the most part, seriously learning swordsmanship today is a very personal undertaking.

In swordsmanship, often what you do not do is almost as important as what you do. Avoiding incorrect form or erroneous technique is a part of developing proper skill. Learn what to do and what not to do. This only comes about through discovering your errors, flaws, and misperceptions. It is a continual process of self-examination. It seems clear that the majority of students of the sword never come close to this attitude in their efforts. Too many, apparently, believe readily enough that they know it all or that there isn't any "higher level" of learning to be achieved. How very wrong they are.

Sadly, many historical fencing enthusiasts today are more interested in playing at swords than in developing historical martial skill or engaging in serious competitions. It is only through disciplined, serious sparring against others that understanding can be gained in striking, parrying, and moving in any form of sword fight. However, swordsmanship is not just applying technique; it is also a creative, intuitive interaction (physical and mental). It is necessary to comprehend both the value and the limitations of techniques. Once this is achieved, actual skill in swordsmanship begins.

Skill cannot be acquired from a mere book. It has to be gained through hands-on learning and sparring. Books can supplement, they can augment, but they cannot themselves instruct. It is through comparison with others and through contrast with their skills that we come to know ourselves. Of course, training and practice require motivation, particularly when we do so alone or without benefit of a traditional, established school, master, or group. It is motivation that pushes us to discover and extend our own physical and mental limits.

Most people are influenced by external motivations (those things that are immediate and tangible), such as avoiding pain, looking good, or gaining prestige. Some people require structure or competition or instant reward in order to be motivated. Others need only direction and aim. Attaining higher skill in swordsmanship, as with other martial arts, eventually requires internal motivation, which is deeper and more personal. It compels a person to compete against himself rather than others and to excel. You train and practice to improve yourself, not to impress others or defeat and ruin them. This kind of internal motivation is uncommon and not found on the more or less superficial levels most practitioners train. Going beyond this is what the higher level of swordsmanship teaches and why it is a creative art that can affect (and improve) one's consciousness.

In swordsmanship, it has been said that the true opponent is, and always has been, one's own self—one's ego, fears, and inadequacies. These are what must be overcome and defeated. After this, any other adversary will fail handily. But it is an endless struggle because perfection is a path, not a destination.

Advice to Readers

For practitioners training in swordsmanship today, the following advice is offered:

1. *Question everything.* No one has all the answers and you should suspect any group, organization, or individual that proclaims or just implies that it does. Even when a particular theory or technique seems fully established and valid, there can always be exceptions or flaws in it. The best way to proceed is to assume that everything is tentative and to always be ready and willing to continually reexamine ideas.

2. *Cross-train.* Whatever form of historical fencing you are pursuing, realize that training is a continual, never-ending process. Seek out as many varieties and methods of swordsmanship and weapon sparring as you can find. Almost any method has some virtues to offer, and practicing exclusively with one method is limiting. Always endeavor to engage as many sparring partners as you can, particularly the better ones. The better the opponent, the more you will be challenged and the more you will learn about yourself. Training with inferior opponents will not bring you to your highest level and can even lead to lazy habits. Do not neglect either sparring or live-blade practice

3. *Research.* Read and study everything you can find on the subject and pay special attention to the works of the classical masters. Don't exclude the wealth of information available in either sport fencing or the modern Asian martial arts. But don't forget that to question and inquire is part of our Western heritage.

4. *Practice.* Although it's a cliché, the three most important things in gaining true skill with the sword are practice, practice, and more practice! Also, there is really no substitute for proper fencing instruction. Find a good, qualified coach for collegiate fencing and stay long enough to actually learn how to fence. Don't treat it as a short-

term activity. But remember, what is taught in sport fencing is not the historical reality. Whether or not such instruction is available, there are still numerous exercises, drills, and routines that should be followed.

Some rudimentary suggestions for rapier training include the following:

- Practice thrusts.
- Practice footwork (for speed, agility, and mobility).
- Practice lunges and recovering.
- Practice point control at a fixed target.
- Practice parry-and-riposte combinations with and without a partner (to gain coordination and reflexes).
- Conduct constant sparring (the only way to learn timing, perception, proper movement, and feedback).
- Train with and without a secondhand weapon (e.g., dagger, buckler).
- Practice some with the sword held in the other hand.
- Practice with a single dagger against a single dagger and against a rapier and dagger.
- Practice routines with a historically accurate replica blade.
- Do some aerobic exercise for stamina.
- Do some form of weight training for strength.
- Practice cut-and-thrust swordsmanship.

The following are suggestions for rudimentary cut-and-thrust training:

- Practice cuts and strikes (for proper delivery, angle, flow, and recovery).
- Practice steps and footwork.
- Practice parry-and-riposte. combinations with and without a partner.
- Practice use and coordination of a second weapon (e.g, buckler, dagger).

- Practice full-contact strikes at a fixed soft target or pell (for power and focus).
- Practice controlled strikes and cuts at a fixed and a mobile target.
- Conduct contact sparring with safe, weapons (padded, wooden, or steel weapons and proper protection).
- Spar at the full body target, including the lower legs.
- Practice with a single sword alone without any buckler or dagger.
- Practice against (and with) pole weapons and larger shields.
- Practice routines with a historically accurate replica.
- Conduct test-cutting with a live blade (to understand how it's supposed to work).
- Do some aerobic exercise for stamina.
- Do some form of weight training for strength.
- Practice rapier fencing.

• • •

Finding sparring opponents who match your ability level can be difficult. Quite often they are either noticeably superior or inferior. Although you may practice with individuals you can readily defeat, it is important not to allow yourself to become lax. You must resist the feeling to fight "softer" or to quit trying in an effort to somehow make things more interesting and challenging. This attitude not only does a disservice to your true skills, but also to your sparring partner by not offering him an honest test. Practice like this leads to bad habits and weakens your edge.

This is not to say that when facing inferior partners you should always crush and overwhelm them. Not at all. In those cases, you obviously need to teach and instruct without diminishing an individual or breaking his spirit. On the other hand, if you face superior partners, you must avoid the urge to view the contest solely in terms of something you failed to do or merely something the opponent did. Victory or defeat is always a combination of what you do or fail to do and what an adversary does or fails to do. Sometimes the two are indistinguishable.

As I keep reiterating, swordsmanship is a path, not a destination. Keep in mind that although there are certain universal concepts of fighting (i.e., perception, distance, timing, technique), every method of swordsmanship or weapon use has its own historical context. No one style or form should be viewed as a be all or end all. It is as much mental (psychological) as physical. Above all should be the realization that this activity takes discipline and physical conditioning—it does not work well with a light-hearted, weekend-pastime approach. It is a martial art and should be treated as such. If you begin to feel inadequate or lacking in skill, this is a good sign; it means you are honestly recognizing that you could be better and that there is more to higher skill than you yet know. The desire to improve is a further step down the path.

It has been said that the true purpose of swordsmanship is the destruction of the ego, of the self, and that it is intended to improve the character of the person wielding the sword. In the words of a famous samurai, "If you would seek skill in the sword, first seek sincerity of the heart, for the former is but a reflection of the latter." If you get nothing else out of this work, let it be this.

Bibliography

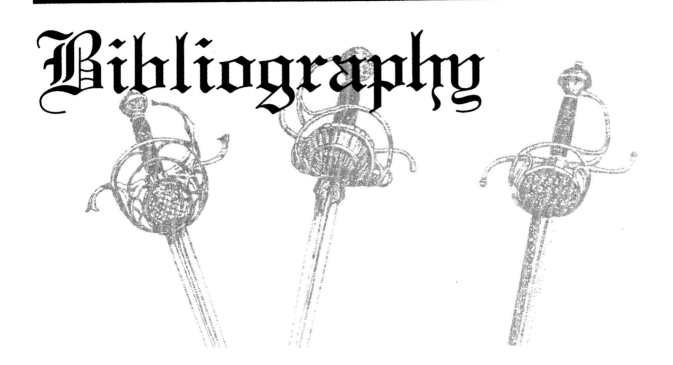

PRIMARY SOURCES AND SUGGESTED READING

Aylward, J.D. *The English Master at Arms from the Twelfth to the Twentieth Century*. London: Routledge and K. Paul, 1956.

Baldick, Robert. *The Duel: A History of Dueling*. Spring Books, 1965.

Bull, Stephen. *An Historical Guide to Arms and Armor*. New York: Facts on File, 1991.

Castle, Egerton. *Schools and Masters of Fence: From the Middle Ages to the Eighteenth Century*. London, 1885.

Cole, Michael D. et. al. *Swords and Hilt Weapons*. London: Weidenfeld and Nicholson, Multimedia Books, 1989.

Limburg, Peter. *What's in a Name of Antique Weapons*. New York: Coward, McCann, and Geoghegan, 1973.

Norman, A.V.B. *The Rapier and Small-Sword 1460–1820*. New York: Arno Press Inc., 1980.

Oakeshott, R.E. *European Weapons and Armour*. Guildford and London: Lutterworth Press, 1980.

Tarrasuk, Leonid. *The Complete Encyclopedia of Arms and Armor*. New York: Simon and Schuster, 1982.

Turner, Craig, and Tony Soper. *Methods and Practice of Elizabethan Swordplay*. Carbondale, Ill.: Southern Illinois University Press, 1990.

Wagner, Edward. *Cut and Thrust Weapons*. London: Spring Books, 1967.

Wikinson, Frederick. *Swords and Daggers*. New York: Hawthorne Books, 1967.

Wise, Arthur. *The Art and History of Personal Combat*. London: Hugh Evelyn Ltd., 1971.

Valentine, Eric. *Rapiers, An Illustrated Reference Guide*. Mechanicsburg, Penn.: Stackpole Books, 1968.

SECONDARY SOURCES

Bower, Muriel. *Foil Fencing*. Dubuque, Iowa: William C. Brown Publishers, 1985.

Burton, Sir Richard. *The Book of the Sword*. London, 1884.

Byam, Michelo. *Arms and Armor*. New York: Dorling Kindersley Limited, 1988.

Curry, Nancy. *Fencing*. Pacific Palisades, Calif.: Goodyear, 1969.

The Diagram Group. *Weapons*. New York: Diagram Visual, 1980.

European Weapons and Armor from the Renaissance to the Industrial Revolution. London: Lutterworth Press, 1980.

Gaugler, William. *A Dictionary of Universally Used Fencing Terminology*. Mildbridge, Maine: Laureate Press, 1993.

Hutton, Alfred. *The Sword and the Centuries*. London: Barnes and Noble, reprint 1901.

Jackson, James L. *Three Elizabethan Fencing Manuals*. New York: Delmar, 1972.

Kiernan, V.G. *The Duel in European History: Honor and the Reign of Aristocracy*. London: Oxford University Press, 1989.

Nadi, Aldo. *On Fencing*, New York: G.P. Putnam's Sons. 1943.

Norman, A.V.B., and Don Pottinger. *English Weapons and Warfare*. London: Barnes and Noble, 1966.

North, Anthony. *European Swords*. London: Victoria and Albert Museum, 1982.

Selberg, Charles. *Foil*. University of Calif., Santa Cruz: Addison-Wesley, 1976.

Sports Illustrated. *Sports Illustrated Book of Fencing*. New York: J.B. Lippincott Co., 1962.

Thimm, Carl. *A Complete Bibliography of Fencing and Dueling*. 1896. (Reprint: New York: B. Blom, 1968.)

Weland, Gerald. *A Collector's Guide to Swords, Daggers, and Cutlasses* London: Chartwell Books, 1991.

Wilkinson, Frederick. *Arms and Armor*. London: Hamlyn, 1978.

_____. *Edged Weapons*. London, 1970.

_____. and Robert Latham. *Swords in Colour*. London, 1978.

Wise, Terence. *European Edged Weapons*. London, 1974.

MAJOR WORKS OF THE EUROPEAN SWORD MASTERS

Asterisk (*) indicates more significant works.

Medieval and Cut and Thrust

1380. Hans Lichtenawer. German fechtbuch of 1389 (earliest known).

1410. Fiore di Liberi. Italy, (*Flos Duellatorium*).

1443. Talhoffer. German fechtbuch of 1443 (drawings only).

*1530. Hans Lebkommer. German fectbuch of 1530 (*Der Alten Fecter an fengliche Kunst*).

Cut and Thrust

1531. Di Antonio Manciolino. (*Opera Nova*).

*1550. Achille Marozzo. 1536 (*Il Duello*), (*Opera Nova*).

1550. Francesco Altoni. Italy.

1598 and 1605. George Silver. London. (*Paradoxes of Defense* and *Brief Instructions . . .*).

1602. William Bass. London. (*Sword and Buckler: Or, The Serving-Man's Defence*).

Rapier (and Cut and Thrust)

1553. Camillo Agrippa. (*His Treatise on the Science of Arms with a Philosophical Dialogue*).

1568. J. Descors. France.

1569. Jeronimo De Carranza. Portuguese. (*De La Philosophia de las Armas*).

*1570. Di Grassi. (*His True Arte of Defense*).

*1570. Joachim Meyer. (*kunst der fechtens*).

*1573. Henry de Sainct Didier. France.

*1575. Angelo Vigianni. (*Lo Schermo*).

1580. Lovino, G.A. (*Traité d'Escrime*).

1584. Alfonso Fallopia.

*1595. Vincent Saviolo. (*His Practice in Two Books*).

1597. Sir William Smythe.

1599. D.L.P. De Narvaez. Spain. (*Libro de las Grandezas de la Espada*).

1601. Marco Docciolini. (*Trattato in materia di scherma*).

1606. Nicoletto Giganti. (*Scola overo Teatro*).

*1606. Salvator Fabris. (*Sienz e Practica d'Arme*).

1609. Hieronime Calvacabo. (*Traité . . . des arms*).

1610. da Cagli. Italy.

*1610. Ridolfo Capo Ferro. (*Gran simulacro . . .*).

1612. Jacob Sutor. (*New Kunstliches Fechtbuch*).

1617. Joseph Swetnam. London. (*Schoole of the Noble and Worthy Science of Defence*).

1619. Joachim Koppen. (*Neuer Diskurs . . . Kunst des Fechtens*).

1630. Girard Thibault. (*Académie de L'Esprée*).

1635. Jean Baptiste la Perché Du Coudray. (*L'Exercise des armes . . .*).

1637. Henry Hexam. London. *Principle of the Art Militairie*).

1639. G.A. London. (*Pallas Armata*. The Gentleman's Armory).

1640/1653. Francesco Alfieri. (*La Sherma* and *La Spadone*).

Small Sword (Excluding Works after Domenico Angelo)

1660. Alessandro Sennesio. (*Il vero maneggio della Spada*).

1663. Besnard. (*Le Maistre d'Armes: Liberal*).

1670. Gieseppi Pallavicini. (*La Scherma Illustra*).

1670. Philibert de la Touche. (*Les Vrays Principes de l'espee seule*).

1676. Jean Baptiste Le Perché. (*L'exercise des armes au le maniment du fleuret*).

1686. Antonio Marcelli. (*Regole Della Scherma*).

1686. André Liancour. (*Le Maistre d'armes*).

1710. Sir William Hope. Scottish. Many works from 1687–1725. (*The Complete Fencing Master*, 1710).

1692. Monssieur L. Abbat. (*Le Maitre D'Armes ou L'exercise de L'espee Seule*).

1696. Bondi Di Mazo. (Spain) (*La Spada Maestra*).

1705. Henry Blackwell. (*The English Fencing Master*).

1711. Z. Wylde. (*The English Master of Defense*).

1728. McBane, Donald. (*The Expert Sword-Man's Companion*).

1740. P. Girard. (*Traite des Armes*).

1763. Domenico Angelo. (*The Schoole of Fencing . . .*).

Period Works on the Code of Dueling

1528. Baldassare Castiglione. (Italy). (*The Courtier*).

1591. Bertrand de Longue. (*Discourses of Warre and Single Combat*).

1599. Sir William Segar. (*The Book of Honor and Arms*).

1606. Lodowick Bryskett. (*A Discourse on Civil Life*).

1617. Vital D'Audiguler. (*Le vray et ancien usage des duels*).

1610. John Selden. (*The Duel, or Single Combat*).

About the Author

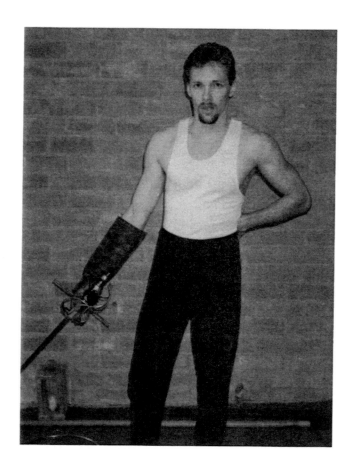

John Clements has had a lifelong pursuit of (some would say obsession with) nearly all forms of swordsmanship. He started fencing at the age of 14 and followed that with an interest in kenjutsu and martial arts. He has been practicing cut-and-thrust swordsmanship for more than 14 years and was a founding member of the Florida Medieval Battling Club (MBC). He taught two semesters on swordsmanship and medieval battling at Western Nevada Community College and took first place in the Advanced Weapon Sparring competition of the U.S. National Kung Fu tournament, in Orlando, Florida, in September 1994. John is an ardent promoter of contact-weapon sparring and historical replica swords. He continues his study of swordsmanship with the new Historical Armed Combat Association (HACA). He currently trains in two-sword, sword-and-shield, and rapier-and-dagger methods.